Profiles

Profiles
24 New Zealand Potters

Cecilia Parkinson & John Parker

dlb *David Bateman*
Auckland

Copyright © Cecilia Parkinson and
John Parker 1988
First published in 1988 by
David Bateman Ltd,
'Golden Heights', 32–34 View Road,
Glenfield, Auckland,
New Zealand

ISBN 0 908610 79 3

Typeset in Helvetica by Lazerprintz
Printed in Hong Kong by
Everbest Printing Co. Ltd

Design — Errol McLeary

Contents

CHESTER NEALIE WOODFIRED POT

JEAN HASTEDT BOX WITH BAMBOO TRIM ▷

Foreword

In 1987 I had the opportunity to be involved with the selection and presentation of the New Zealand Society of Potters' annual exhibition displayed at the Sarjeant Gallery in Wanganui in May. It was very clear from that exhibition, and others which I have seen over recent years, that studio ceramics are firmly established in New Zealand.

One exciting aspect of this is that such work no longer consists of pondering, 'one-off' art pieces made by very able functional potters as they struggle to approach unclear art-gallery expectations. Rather, these are the creations of artists who see their studio pieces as their mainstream work. This important development has been liberating not only for those who wish to explore the possibilities of using clay in new ways, but also for those who have the skills and attitude to reinforce and extend the functional quality and traditions of the medium.

Of course, much of the work that is being produced by this new wave of ceramic artists has yet to be resolved in terms of the additional aesthetic assessments which need to be applied to it as it starts to fill the vacuum which has long existed in the country's museum collections. This lack of institutional appreciation can be seen as but one example of how uncomfortable and frequently wide is the chasm which exists between the functional and the so-called 'fine' arts here. In New Zealand historically we have given scant consideration to the applied and decorative arts and within our public collections they have mostly been treated as having less importance than the fine arts.

Fortunately all of this has been changing as artists in many media have started producing work that challenges the unacceptably narrow categories of museum collections. One result has been a necessary breaking down of barriers so that it is now possible to assess work in the context of its intentions and the quality of its achievements relevant to that, instead of having it merely categorised by medium or process.

While institutions are always slow to respond to these changes, some reassessment is now clearly taking place and this is particularly evident in their approach to Maori material. As the energy of all artists working in that ground between entrenched categories, not only in clay but in a wide range of other media, continues to produce challenging and worthwhile work, galleries will need to shape fresh collecting policies to better respond to it.

Along with these changes, however, it will be necessary for the work being produced to be assessed on how successfully it meets its intentions. Its relevance to other work with the same intentions in other media must also be considered. For example, work which is exploring sculptural issues should first stand or fall on its success as a sculpture. The work that is decorative must be considered in terms of other decorative works in other media. The conceptual work will need to be assessed in terms of the strengths of the concepts. This is a liberating and challenging opportunity for the artists generally and particularly for those who are endeavouring to extend their work through a specific medium like clay.

It is already clear to me from recent exhibitions and the interesting cross-section of profiles in this book that the potential is now open for ceramic artists with this exciting new energy to take a mainstream position within the visual arts in New Zealand.

I am pleased to have this opportunity to briefly contribute to this important first in a series on New Zealand potters. I congratulate Cecilia and John on their efforts and David Bateman Ltd on their commitment and support of the visual arts.

Bill Milbank,
Director,
Sarjeant Gallery,
Wanganui, December 1987

Introduction

The Studio Pottery Movement in New Zealand has been an extraordinary growth phenomenon.
Until the early 1970s there had been no formal tertiary craft education available in this area. In 1979, Census statistics showed that in a country with a population of around three million, there were 44,000 people actively engaged in pottery; 5000 of these were considered professional potters.

The making of pottery came to New Zealand with nineteenth-century European colonisation. A developing country needed drainage pipes and bricks. Geographical isolation being the mother of invention, by the 1870s utilitarian and ornamental pottery was being produced. Early studio potters, like Briar Gardner in the 1920s, were associated with the knowledge and technology of the existing brickworks. Others such as Robert Field and Olive Jones returned to New Zealand in 1934 with British art-school training and Stoke-on-Trent experience.

Early studio potters were largely self taught through Bernard Leach's classic, *A Potter's Book* (1939). Kilns were Heath-Robinson affairs of recycled bricks and fired with diesel and old vacuum cleaners. It was a time of pioneer enthusiasm and shared experience. The virtues of no formal training produced a breed of blood-and-guts potters, passionate individuals in the best do-it-yourself tradition.

From the late forties enthusiasts introduced pottery into art and craft teacher training. By 1957 there were sufficient potters for Oswald Stephens to organise the first exhibition of New Zealand studio potters in the Otago Museum.

Bernard Leach's St Ives Pottery in Cornwall, Michael Cardew's workshop in Abuja in Nigeria and Hamada's studio at Mashiko in Japan became essential stopovers for New Zealanders seeking overseas experience. Night-school classes in pottery flourished and most shopping centres had their craft shop as well as their butcher, chemist, newsagent and dairy.

The seventies saw the craft revival and the Studio Pottery Movement at their height, with the help of import restrictions. The rejection of commercial and industrial styles and standards of the previous generation was complete.

Since the mid seventies, work has radically diversified. The newest generation, perhaps reacting against the homespun, handcrafted lifestyles of their sixties' parents, have provided the right aesthetic and financial climate for an interest in fine porcelain and glass to flourish. There has also been an overdue renewed interest in earthenware, once the maligned preserve of the amateur.

The isolation argument no longer applies. New Zealanders are great travellers and big on overseas experience. They are one of the greatest consumers of books and magazines in the world. What is happening anywhere has a publication delay of three months at the most.

New Zealand is no longer one of the best kept secrets in the world.

CAMPBELL HEGAN OVOID AND BLOSSOM POT

JOHN PARKER BOWL, 1987

CATHERINE ANSELMI

I was brought up on a remote farm in Waikawau Valley on the west coast about 50 km north of New Plymouth. That's where the real beaches are, empty and rugged, with blue-black sand.

In 1979 I began working with porcelain, and I wanted to do something really drastic with it, maybe as a reaction to the high-fired celadon things people were then doing. This led to me making low-fired smoked raku porcelain bowls. These were very fragile and provoked an extreme reaction. In 1981 I bought a house in Auckland at Epsom with a group of friends and established a studio-workshop. There I reacted against a demand for my work by not doing any! Later I began working in secret, experimenting with hand-building, impressing shell images and inlaying vitreous slips. In 1984 I became involved in working with tukutuku panels and began for the first time using another material and incorporating it with clay.

Because I was spending so much time exploring new directions while at the same time trying to make a living from potting, it now seemed that I required an income area which would leave the new work free to go wherever it needed. I no longer wanted to retail through traditional pottery outlets, so I began to develop a range of slip-cast terracotta pieces which I could sell through interior-design stores.

I am now producing two ranges of slip-cast ware. One is of burnished, low-fired terracotta, some of which, once fired, are left in the terracotta colour, and some of which are blackened in a further smoke firing. A subsequent range is of white clay pieces which are bisque-fired at 1100°C, with matt glazes applied for a second firing at 1000°C.

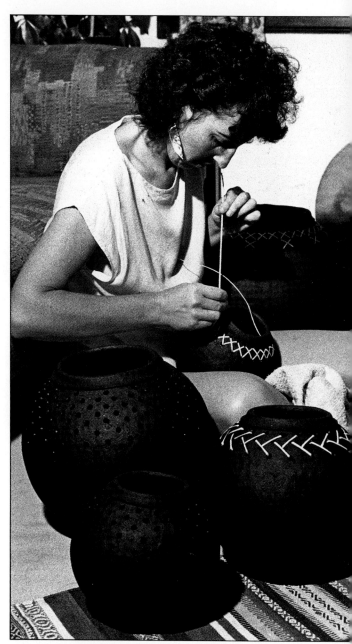

PHOTO — ANNA CAMPBELL

Catherine Anselmi

BIOGRAPHY

1953 Born New Plymouth
1967 Went to boarding school in Auckland
1972 Studied one term at Auckland University, which convinced me I didn't want to do that
1972–6 Trained as a psychiatric nurse at Oakley and Carrington hospitals, Auckland
1976 Daughter Janai born
1977 Began making pots after six months of being a parent. Studied with Pat Perrin at the Auckland Studio Potters Centre. I bought a wheel, and every time Janai went to sleep, I would make pots.
1978 Continued studying with John Parker for a second year. From then I was shown the confidence to bypass the traditional domestic-ware apprenticeship which it was assumed all potters had to do
1978–81 Did my country service, and was almost self-sufficient in a worker's cottage on the family farm
1981 Moved back to Auckland city and set up studio-workshop with friends

Exhibitions
1979 Group raku exhibition, Albany Village Pottery, Auckland
1980– Auckland Studio Potters annual exhibitions
1981 Alicat Gallery, Auckland
1981–2 Exhibited annually, Fletcher Brownbuilt Pottery Award, Auckland
1985 Pots of Ponsonby, Auckland
1987 Winstone Craft Biennale, Auckland

Collections
Auckland Studio Potters
Auckland Institute and Museum

Slip-cast lamp base production line
PHOTOS — JOHN McNICOL

◁ LAMP BASE, 1987
White clay, bisque fired to 1100˚C,
with matt glaze applied for second
firing to 1000˚C
PHOTO — PAUL SOWRY

LAMP BASE, 1987 ▷
White clay, bisque fired to 1100˚C,
with matt glaze applied for second
firing to 1000˚C
PHOTO — PAUL SOWRY

◁ LAMP BASE, 1987
Slip-cast burnished terracotta, low
bisque fired and blackened in a
further smoke firing
PHOTO — PAUL SOWRY

THREE LACED VESSELS, 1986 ▷
Largest piece, diameter — 37 cm;
height — 28 cm. Coiled and
pinched, smoked, laced with kiekie.
PHOTO — HOWARD WILLIAMS

ANNEKE BORREN

I have been working in New Zealand for the last 17 years as a professional potter. My background and interests in clay shapes are influenced by Scandanavian design, a clarity of execution and complementary decoration, emphasising the graphic quality of my work — though I do feel influenced by New Zealand and identify with it.

After having explored colourful high-fired earthenware as well as majolica-type brushed stoneware, always in oxidation firings, I've been working over the last two years with an iron-rich glaze with black-on-black brushwork decoration fired to 1290°C. The decoration fluid consists of an overdose of oxides which crystallise out on the surface and therefore creates a silvery-grey sheen with light falling on it. The effect looked for is the subtlety of blending in and standing out.

The use of black bamboo, which we grow in the garden, is a complementary design feature which I like exploring further. Another combination is the use of bone, whalebone and ivory in the form of carvings by my husband, Owen Mapp, as feature lids of the pots and sometimes doubling as pendants. The contrasts between the dark and light forces one to evaluate both shapes.

I work in a studio adjoining the house, with skylights and big sliding doors, overlooking the garden. In it are two electric kilns, dimensions 7.5 and 2.5 cu. ft. When I'm experimenting with glazes, my shortest run of clay to finished product is four days. This means the continuity of thought and action is fairly unbroken and new ideas and forms come through fast.

I work on an electric wheel but mostly on an old-fashioned Danish kickwheel, at which I am half standing, half sitting, and on which I do all my freehand brushwork on the pots. My fascination with interlocking circles on rounded shapes is endless and the rhythm of such brushwork very soothing.

Emotionally I identify very strongly with the subtleties of my black glaze, as over the last three years I've been working mostly at night, with artificial light flooding the

PHOTO — HELEN MITCHELL

darkness, while our children are small and my days are filled with them.

In 1986 I changed over to a gas-fired kiln to explore reduction glazes. I still do all my work on the wheel. The unending turning of clay and days is a continual learning process.

BIOGRAPHY

1946 Born in Eindhoven, Holland
1963 Emigrated to New Zealand
1965 Started fulltime potting in the backyard
1966 Study year, School of Fine Arts, Ilam, Christchurch
1967–9 Ceramic study tour of Europe and USA, including:
1 year in the Experimental Department of the Porceleyne Fles, Delft, Holland, with tuition from Lily ter Kuile and ceramist Emmy van Deventer;
3 months work in Denmark with Kahler Keramic Fabrik, a fourth-generation family factory of handmade ceramics;
10 months in Sweden at the Industrial School of Arts in Gothenberg
1969 Set up own studio in Paraparaumu
1971 Married Owen Mapp, sculptor-carver
Member of NZ Potters Guild
Member of the NZ Society of Potters
Member of the NZ Chapter of the World Crafts Council
1977 Commissioned by the NZ Government to design and execute ceramics for Parliament's new Beehive building
1979 Studied crystalline glazes under Jack Boydston, Santa Barbara, Calif., USA
Gave birth to Tahi in California
Included in Sotheby's auction of Delft ceramics in Amsterdam, Holland
1981 Gave birth to Tamara in New Zealand

Exhibitions
1969– Solo and group shows in most of the main museums and galleries throughout New Zealand
South Pacific Arts Festival, Fiji
Australia
Rheinischen Landes Museum, Bonn
Los Angeles Folk and Craft Museum, Calif., USA
Running Ridge Gallery, Ojai, Calif., USA
Yes Store, Santa Barbara, Calif., USA
Mississippi Crafts International, Jackson, Miss., USA
1983–5 Exhibited annually, Fletcher Brownbuilt Pottery Award, Auckland
1984 Solo show with Owen Mapp, Otago Museum, Dunedin
1985 *Black and White Show* with Robyn Stewart and Owen Mapp, Dowse Art Gallery, Lower Hutt
Solo show with Owen Mapp, Albany Village Pottery, Auckland
1986 Solo show with Owen Mapp, Gallery 242, Hastings

Awards
1984 Winner, NatWest Craft Award, NZ Academy of Fine Arts, Wellington

Collections
NZ Government touring exhibitions
Auckland Institute and Museum
Hawkes Bay Art Gallery and Museum, Napier
Southland Museum, Invercargill
Otago Museum, Dunedin
Dowse Art Gallery, Lower Hutt
Museum of Applied Arts and Technology, Sydney
Museum Booymans van Beuningen, Rotterdam, Holland
NZ Embassies

Publications
Craft New Zealand, Doreen Blumhardt and Brian Brake, Wellington, 1981
Please Touch, Peter Cape, Auckland, 1980
Three Hundred Years of Delft Ceramics, and *The History of the Delft Factory*, The Porceleyne Fles, Delft, Holland

Featured in the NZ National Film Unit documentaries *A Sense of Involvement* and *Crafts in New Zealand*

◁ BONE-LIDDED POTS, 1985
Sizes range from: height — 33 to
17 cm; width — 8 to 9 cm. Brush
decorated overglazed stoneware,
fired at 1290˚C. Lids of lathed bone
by Owen Mapp.
PHOTO — HELEN MITCHELL

BAMBOO POT, 1985 △
Height — 26 cm; width — 22 cm.
Brush-decorated overglazed
stoneware. Fired at 1290˚C. Black
bamboo lid.
PHOTO — HELEN MITCHELL

TOTEM POLES, 1985 ▷
Sizes range from: height — 49 to
33 cm; width — 37 to 28 cm.
Brush-decorated overglazed
stoneware, fired at 1290˚C. Black
bamboo insertions.
PHOTO — HELEN MITCHELL

◁ BAMBOO POT, 1985
Height — 36 cm; width — 18 cm.
Brush-decorated overglazed
stoneware. Fired at 1290˚C. Black
bamboo lid.
PHOTO — HELEN MITCHELL

SUE CLIFFORD

PHOTO — ANN CLIFFORD

The philosophy behind my work is to project something of myself; images held deep within my soul, whether it be those built of the past, or that which surrounds me in the present time. To shut out all that intrudes on my thoughts and take a long searching look at myself and what I hold important. To dismiss those influences which others would force upon me, whether they be in lifestyle, perception or thought, or, the most arrogant of all, the type of work I should produce.

I have never made domestic ware. I'm not a domestic sort of person. To me the whole concept lacks depth, both in thought and the perception of our surroundings as a whole.

I have long been fascinated by night with its ethereal, elusive qualities setting land-scapes awash with shades of blue-black; a large, soft blanket that quietens all to the subtlety it demands; the moon rolling among dark clouds, casting a rainbow halation through the mists when they part to let it through; closing again to let it carry on along its own private journey.

In the series illustrated here it has been my objective to capture the haunting qualities of dreams. Fleeting images through an unknown past to an ever present future. Unseeing night-birds, suspended in that magical instant where night transforms into day, caught up in their web of ever shifting constellations which carry them forth in endless migration to yet another night. Base-born, yet with the ability to soar above all humanity, ever searching to find the spirit they once had, to free themselves from the corruption of Man's refuse. A journey through the dream realms of night, governed by the subconscious which only too often hides from the stark light of day.

The 'Disintegration' forms are representative of that which remains after sleep has passed, like the kelp roots that remain on the shore after the night tide has returned to its hidden depths, solid images which provide hints of the dream realm behind them.

BIOGRAPHY
1958 Born Dunedin
Self-taught potter
Eight years' fulltime potting, with emphasis on porcelain

Exhibitions
1979–87 Numerous exhibitions around New Zealand
1982 40th Concorso Internazionalle della Ceramica d'Arte, Faenza, Italy
1983 41st Concorso Internazionalle della Ceramica d'Arte, Faenza, Italy
1984 *Arredo Urbano*, Italy
1986 *Triennale de la Porcelain*, Nyon, Switzerland (Out of the 16 selected, the only person residing in the Southern Hemisphere)

Awards
1980 Merit Award winner, Fletcher Brownbuilt Pottery Award, Auckland

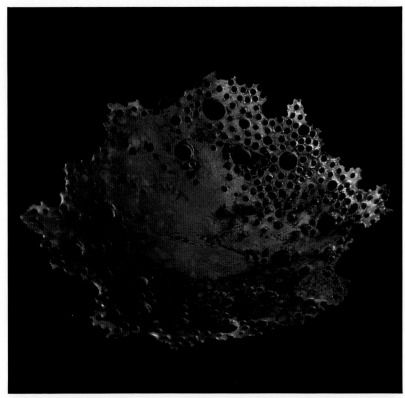

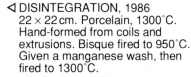

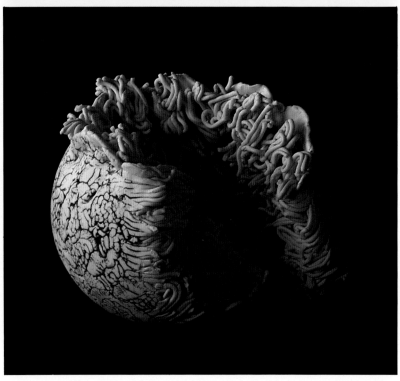

◁ FRAGMENTED NIGHT, 1986
9 × 9 × 4 cm. Porcelain, 1330°C.
Pinched bowl form, pierced when
leather-hard. Bisque fired to 950°C.
Glazed in shiny mottle blue-black at
1300°C. Lustre fired to 800°C with
mother of pearl lustre.
PHOTO — ANN CLIFFORD

NIGHT WEB, 1986 ▷
25 × 25 × 7.5 cm. Porcelain,
1300°C. Pinched base, pierced in
leather-hard state. Bisque fired to
950°C. Glaze fired with navy-blue
shiny glaze to 1300°C. Lustre firing
with deep violet lustre to 800°C.
After final firing the piece was then
threaded with silver wire and the
birds, also porcelain, added at this
stage.
PHOTO — ANN CLIFFORD

◁ DISINTEGRATION, 1986
22 × 22 cm. Porcelain, 1300°C.
Hand-formed from coils and
extrusions. Bisque fired to 950°C.
Given a manganese wash, then
fired to 1300°C.
PHOTO — ANN CLIFFORD

NIGHT DESCENDING, 1986 ▷
30 × 30 × 12 cm. Porcelain,
1300°C. Pinched base, pierced in
leather-hard state. Top section of
base also pinched and pierced at
leather-hard state. Bisque fired
separately to 950°C. The upper
section was given a wash of matt
black satin while the lower section
was glazed in a shiny deep navy
glaze. The pieces were then
assembled and fired to 1300°C to
allow the glaze to bind them
together, after which the piece was
given two separate lustre firings to
800°C, one with mottled deep violet
and the other with mother of pearl.
After the final firing the base was
threaded with silver wire and the
birds were added.
PHOTO — ANN CLIFFORD

22

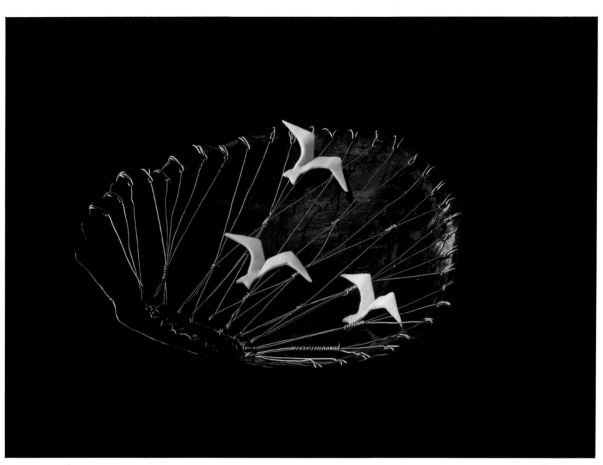

JOHN CRAWFORD

My studio objectives are to explore the aesthetic qualities of clay through a process of constant involvement. Working with clay has always obsessed me. I cannot imagine doing anything else.

Recent work from 1981 to 1985 has evolved into a series of figurative works loosely titled 'Body Language'. My fascination with the human form and its integration into a three-dimensional object that also speaks of the 'making process' and of glaze and clay, has set a challenge I feel I will not exhaust in a lifetime. Starting points for works have come from such things as newspaper fashion clippings, cubist painting, abstract expressionism and the 'making process', to name a few.

Working drawings play an important role in reinforcing the concept before committing myself to clay. They also serve as useful reference points for the development of new works. Over the past two years I have gradually introduced the use of on-glaze enamels to my works, giving an added colour dimension. For me, 1987 has continued to see the development of the figurative and a number of symbols have evolved and become predominant in my work. They include red cats and green and blue female figures.

The building up of experience through constant involvement has been a crucial factor in my learning. Attending the first Australian National Ceramics Symposium in Canberra was an important point in the development of my work. New areas of interest involve the development of low-fired glazes in oxidising atmospheres.

Concepts I would like my work to aspire to involve a sense of caring and craftsmanship in pieces that make a visual statement related to line, colour and form.

PHOTO — MARGARET HOWARD

BIOGRAPHY

1951 Born on the West Coast, South Island
1974 Completed 5 years with Waimea Craft Pottery, Nelson. This involved intensive training in wheelwork skills, glazing and firing techniques, in a 'Leach-style' studio workshop. Established own studio at Hector, 30 km north of Westport, with wife Anne, who also completed her training at Waimea
1985–8 President, NZ Society of Potters
1986 NZ guest potter at 1st National Australian Ceramics Symposium, Canberra

Exhibitions

1970– NZ Society of Potters annual exhibitions
1974 Suter Art Gallery, Nelson
1975 NZ Academy of Fine Arts annual exhibition
1976 Auckland Studio Potters annual exhibition
1980 Exhibitor, Fletcher Brownbuilt Pottery Award, Auckland
1981 *The Bowl*, Crafts Council of New Zealand exhibition, Wellington
1983 *The Great New Zealand Box Show*, Crafts Council of NZ exhibition, Wellington
1983– Exhibited annually, Fletcher Brownbuilt Pottery Award, Auckland
World Crafts exhibition, Canada
1985 New Zealand House, London
Winstone Ties That Bind, Crafts Council of NZ exhibition, Wellington
Sarjeant Gallery, Wanganui
1986 *Earth and Fire*, Southern Regional Arts Council touring exhibition
New Zealand Potters, Gallery Eight, La Jolla, California
Out of New Zealand, exhibition at Santa Barbara Film Festival, Calif., USA
Pacific Link, Expo '86, Richmond Art Gallery, Vancouver, Canada
Canberra Art Gallery, Australia
Ceramics '86, Govett-Brewster Gallery, New Plymouth
Spheres, NZ Society of Potters exhibition, Southland Museum, Invercargill
1987 Winstone Craft Biennale, Auckland

Collections

ANZ Bank, Wellington
Korean Embassy
NZ Ministry of Foreign Affairs, Paris
Southland Art Gallery, Invercargill
Suter Art Gallery, Nelson
Auckland Studio Potters collection, Auckland Institute and Museum
QEII Arts Council, Christchurch
Sir Ronald Scott private collection, Christchurch
Myers Foundation, Australia
Winstone Ltd, Auckland

'PAIR WITH BATHERS' — △
BODY-LANGUAGE VASES
18.5 × 15 cm and 15 × 12.5 cm.
Porcelain. On-glaze lips.
PHOTO — MARGARET HOWARD

'PEOPLE WITHIN PEOPLE' ▽
87 × 30 × 13 cm. Porcelain
sculpture bolted together. On-glaze
enamels.
PHOTO — MARGARET HOWARD

GROUP OF THREE ▷
BODY-LANGUAGE JUGS
Largest 61 × 20 × 11 cm.
Stoneware. Fired 1280°C with
on-glaze enamels.
PHOTO — MARGARET HOWARD

STEVE FULLMER

When I first came to New Zealand in 1973 I knew how to centre a ball of clay and enough to wipe the clay off my hands before I ate my sandwich.

Peter Beach of Beach Artware, Henderson, gave me my first actual job where I would get paid to make pots and repair and maintain electric kilns. The first week I didn't get paid, but usually watched Dan Steenstra make pots and then would go off to my wheel to give it a turn. By the second week I was on the payroll. It was a great job and I owe Peter a lot for being so generous and helpful. By the end of 1974 I had decided to emigrate to New Zealand. While this was being processed I toured Australia.

In Australia I landed another production-throwing job with Courtland Pottery in Perth, a big earthenware pottery. On my return to New Zealand in 1975 I worked again for Peter Beach alongside Dan Steenstra, but it wasn't the same. I was changing. I was really starting to notice other potters' work and had visited their workshops. The lifestyle of these self-employed potters really influenced my quitting production work. Production throwing is a valuable experience to have, no doubt in my mind. To have had the experience of working alongside the skilled hands of Dan Steenstra was a tremendous opportunity — he's the greatest thrower I've ever seen.

In 1976 I moved to Nelson to establish my own workshop. It was rough going at first. I had built a 100 cu. ft. Dutch oven that couldn't reach cone 9, so for the first six months I only made terracotta planters and crocks that no one would buy because they had no glaze inside or out. The coarse granite I used as grog didn't help the matter at all. Eventually I got my kiln to work wonderfully and between 1976-9 I was making a full range of domestic ware plus stoneware and earthenware planters.

In 1979 I went with my wife, Robin, to California, where my parents live. We stayed two and a half years. While in California I became very interested in lower firing techniques. The textures and colours

were amazing, to say the least. Also, I was exposed to new types of forms with tremendous power that I had never seen before. I think I was starting to realise that some clay forms were as powerful as any painting I had ever seen. It was art — clay art.

When we finally did come back to Nelson in 1981, I found it really difficult to make the same stuff that I had depended on for so many years. Since then I have incorporated more deliberate art into my pieces. I am no longer a production potter; I work too slowly for that. I usually work with four to six pieces in a series, in different sizes, making them one day, coming back the next day to

BIOGRAPHY
1946 Born in Portland, Oregon, USA
1955 Moved to Baldwin Park, Calif.
1964 Attended art classes at Mt San Antonio Jnr College
1966 Drafted into the US Army; 15 months in Korea
1970 Attended Long Beach Jnr College pottery classes
1973 Working holiday to New Zealand
1974 Permanent resident of New Zealand Production thrower, Beach Artware, Henderson, Auckland
Production thrower, Courtland Pottery, Perth
1976 Set up own workshop in Upper Moutere, Nelson. Built 100 cu. ft. wood-fired kiln
1979 Holiday to USA and Britain
Production thrower, The Studio, Whittier, Calif. Also at Halstead Ceramics, Baldwin Park, Calif.
1979–81 Attended many workshops and schools pertaining to clay
1981 Moved back to Nelson, NZ. Working more at lower temperature firings, developing art pieces
1986 Opened Steve Fullmer Gallery in Tasman, Nelson. Moved to Tasman to develop workshop-studio and build an anagama kiln and two gas-fired brick kilns.

Awards
1985 Merit Award winner, Fletcher Brownbuilt Pottery Award, Auckland
1986 Winner, Fletcher Brownbuilt Pottery Award, Auckland

ALL PHOTOS — STEVE FULLMER

THE MAKING OF A WALKING MUDFISH

1. First step is to have very well wedged clay so as not to have weak spots show up when it is stretched.

I next shape the clay with a hand dough-roller to get the general shape I want, then I stretch the clay in a downward movement to attain the required texture and shape. This shape is left to dry a bit and flipped regularly.

2. Once the body is firm enough to work on, the eyes, mouth and fins are next attached.

3. The legs have had a dowel inserted through the centre to reduce thickness. As well, after the piece has been fired a steel dowel can be used to support the fish in the garden. I do not use water or slip but firmly press the legs on to a well scored area, then shape.

4. Checking to see that the feet are flat for stability. I also put pinholes into the legs to allow moisture out during firing. I usually stand back and have a good look at the personality that has developed in the fish and might now add more texture to it if needed, keeping in mind that a lot can be done with slips and stains.

FIRING INFORMATION

The Walking Mudfish are bisque-fired to 1060 — 1080°C. I then spray or pour on slip. Next I spray on a solution of salt and soda ash plus different sulphates. The fish are then put into my saggars filled with sawdust, bark, salt, sulphates and soda ash. They are fired to 1000 — 1020°C in six hours. I like the fish to look as if they have just 'stepped' out of the mud.

FISH CLAY BODY

Winstone's GB2, medium grog added, or Mac's Mud Co. Waiwhero body, medium grog added.

SLIPS

WHITE
Calcined china clay 30%
Clay 10%
Flint 40%
Colmanite 15%
Add any stain 5 — 20%

FULLMER BLACK SLIP
Mahana clay — terracotta 70%
Manganese dioxide 20%
Black stain 2 — 5%

CALLING WIND, 1986
34 × 36 cm. Low fired lead glaze.

PHOTO — STEVE FULLMER

expand them, making them larger with ribs
or whatever it takes. Sometimes the clay
tears! That's great! I work on each piece
until I get some kind of reaction from it.
Most of my pieces are fired to 1000°C; they
have primitive and fragile qualities.

JAR, 1986 △
42 × 32 cm. Blue slip, low fired.
PHOTO — STEVE FULLMER

WALKING MUDFISH, 1986 ▷
54 × 50 cm. Low fired lead glaze
over black slip.
PHOTO — STEVE FULLMER

GARDEN ON BOWL, 1986 ▽
20 × 50 cm. Low fired lead glaze.
PHOTO — STEVE FULLMER

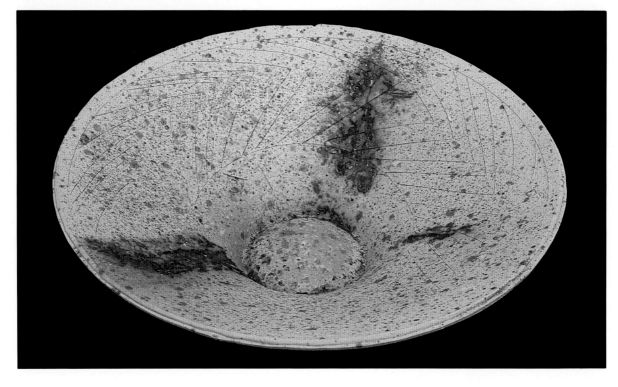

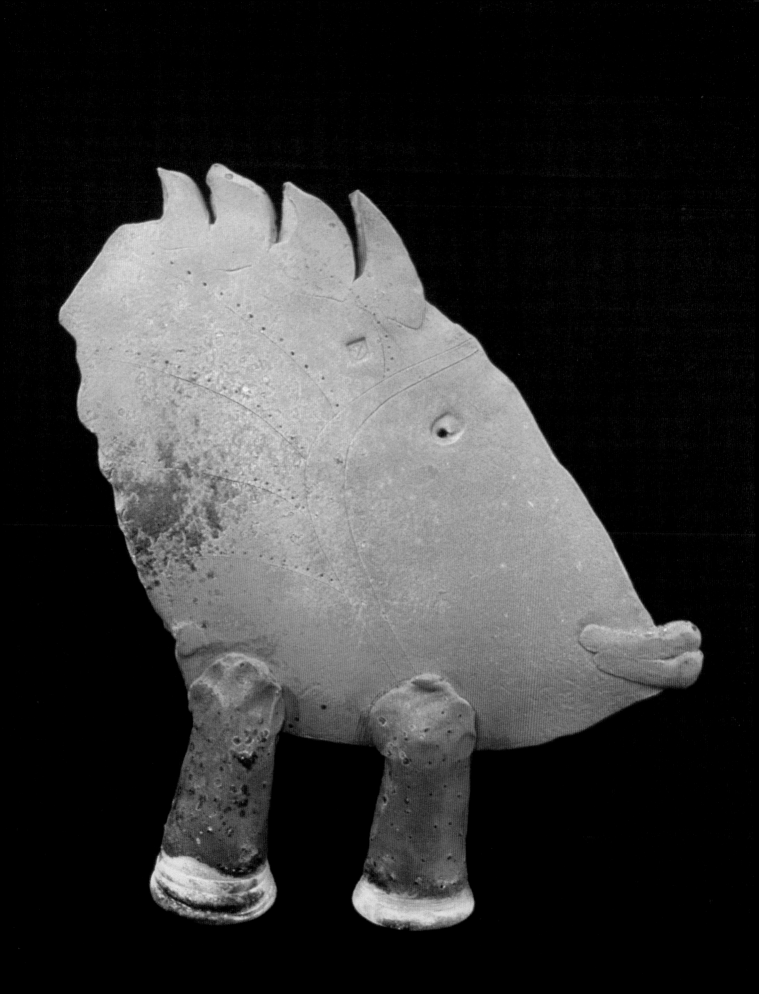

BRIAN GARTSIDE

I was not born in New Zealand — I chose to live here. This country has always impressed me as a very 'geographical' land. Dynamic physical features dominate, agents of erosion are active, and movement and potential change are very evident. Skies, activated by two large oceans, put on a continuous show of powerful, flowing images. There is a scattering of humans living on its surface, creating their hard surfaces and straight lines, enjoying the fluid climate with blues and greens and fast growing vegetation.

I like the idea of being a potter and knowing about glazes and kilns, developing skills like throwing and forming, knowing also that the things I make go into people's homes. I've always felt that I needed to use colour and shapes and even my functional ware is filled with fluid, coloured glazes that enliven the surface.

Because I spent many years teaching in the arts, I learned a lot about clay from my students. They didn't know they were teaching me and for many years I didn't know it either. It took a long time to realise that all the time I was telling people how to do it and how to think about it, I was making a false assumption about learning. All my talking didn't make any difference; people could find their own way and certainly were not experiencing my perceptions.

I've been a very slow learner. Another thing it took a long time to learn was to trust — trust that what I was feeling and doing and making was all right and that comments and reactions from other people only represented opinion. Reviewers and critics merely describe their own perceptions. That seems an easy and obvious thing to say and think, but to really 'know' it makes a tremendous difference as I work. I also now completely trust that the type of art I am most comfortable with is that which comes from a person's own experience and emotion, without a lot of 'borrowing'. When you work with ideas *you* are the one who knows.

Since I gave up teaching I've spent a lot of time talking to myself — sometimes with words but also with shapes and lines —

PHOTO — ROGER HARDIE

BIOGRAPHY

Born Chorley, Lancashire
1960 Studied at Cadley Grammar School, Bristol School of Art, Birmingham School of Art, Dudley College of Education
1966–70 Lecturer in art, Sydney Webb College, London
1970–4 Ardmore Teachers College, Auckland
1975–80 North Shore Teachers College, Auckland
1980– Fulltime, self-employed artist/craftsperson. Has tutored at many residential and weekend workshops around England and New Zealand.
1985 Guest potter, Northern Arizona University, Flagstaff, Arizona, USA
1986 QEII Arts Council grant for a major project

Exhibitions

1971 Academy International Ceramics
1975 New Zealand tour, South-East Asia
1981 39th Concorso Internazionalle della Ceramica d'Arte, Faenza, Italy
1984 New Zealand House, London
Clay and Glass Az Art, Flagstaff, Arizona, USA
1985 International ceramics exhibition, Taipei Fine Arts Museum, Taiwan
1986 Dowse Art Museum, Lower Hutt.
Has regularly participated in invitational exhibitions at major New Zealand and overseas galleries

Collections

Auckland Institute and Museum
Waikato Art Museum, Hamilton
Hawkes Bay Art Gallery and Museum, Napier
Dowse Art Gallery, Lower Hutt
NZ Academy of Fine Arts, Wellington
Fletcher Challenge collection
NZ Ministry of Foreign Affairs collection
Private collections in New Zealand and overseas

Publications

Craft New Zealand, Doreen Blumhardt and Brian Brake, Wellington, 1981
Please Touch, Peter Cape, Auckland, 1980
Potters Manual, Kenneth Clark, UK, 1983

1985 Contributed to National Film Unit feature, *Craft Pride*
1987 Featured in TVNZ 'Kaleidoscope' series

developing a handwriting that only makes sense to itself. I let those conversations scrawl their way across the clay. Every crack, bump, blister and hollow, hard line and dribble, talk to each other. They all seem to tell each other what needs to be done. One colour needs another and so it goes on. Sometimes it seems that the conversation is never ending and I do get the feeling that the pieces are never finished.

Then there is the puzzling feeling that if I'm *mean't* to do a thing a certain way, I can't resist doing it differently. I thought at first that maybe I just didn't like rules, and then I decided that in art you can make your own rules. Another thing that I find is that the so-called 'faults' offer terrific opportunities to be more creative, and more 'mistakes' lead to more learning and progress. Playing around with faults, mistakes, breaking rules and trying opposites, do sometimes lead to awkward and misinterpreted situations. On the other hand, the whole business of trying the opposites and doing things the 'wrong' way nearly always yields results that are demanding and that lead to new ideas that work and also seem more dynamic.

Then there are decisions . . . always torn by decisions — whether to do functional work or Art? Which glaze? Which kiln? Which fuel? High fire or low fire? My answer to myself now is to do both and if there really has to be a choice of one, something very close at hand will be pointing the way. I'm constantly amazed how the clay or the fire tells me which to choose or what to do next.

Making judgments and setting standards seem to prevent and limit. I find it a useful technique to suspend these two activities. There always comes a point when I try to see that there's no value in this piece of clay — it is of no consequence what happens to it. That's when things usually start to happen! Try it. Give it a go! If you don't do it, you'll never know.

I don't think I know what my marks mean, but after evolving over many years, they seem to be a mixture of habit, accident,

33

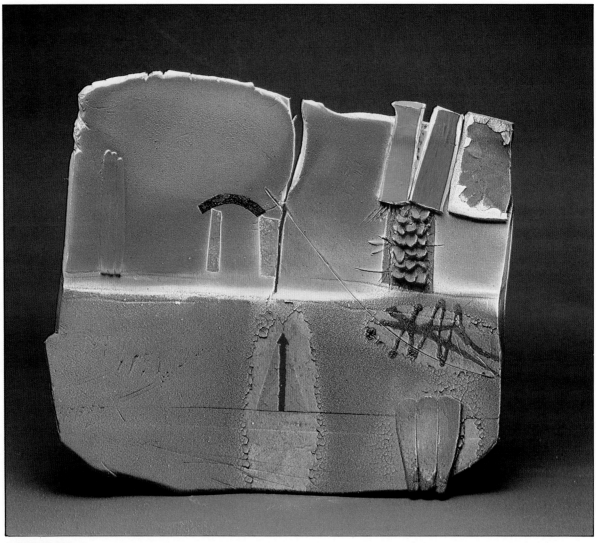

FREEFORM
40 × 50 cm. Multifired glazes, slips
and enamels.
PHOTO — IAN NORMAN

material process and environment. Often I
don't feel a reason for doing something, but
more that it needs to be done. I just do it.

I tend to make simple forms — flat, like
plates or spheres, partial spheres, and
developments of spheres. I proceed to alter,
destroy, repair and transform these quickly-
made objects with surfaces, colours and
marks. It's sometimes hard to say whether
there's any meaning. The marks relate to
the moment, to habit and to each other, and
a few marks definitely relate to remnants of
geographical and meteorological memories.
All manner of techniques are employed —
dribbling, dipping, spraying, brushing,
stencilling, drawing and printing.

To begin with, the colour range was
limited by the fact that I had access to only
the basic oxides like iron and copper. The
colours I learned to obtain were varied but
also limited. Thanks to many circum-
stances, it is now almost possible to acquire
and fire every colour of the spectrum, at
almost any temperature. From my point of
view, it has made possible all kinds of new
developments that help to make my images
stronger and clearer.

I also find that simple combinations of
nepheline syenite, barium carbonate, zinc
oxide, wood ash and the stains make good
basic surfaces on which to perform multiple
firings at different temperatures.

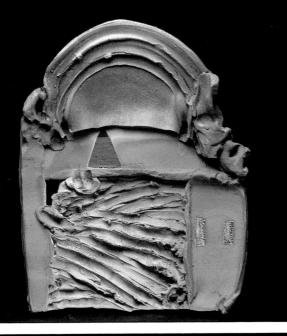

◁ FREEFORM
40 × 50 cm. Multifired glazes, slips
and enamels.
PHOTO — IAN NORMAN

SQUARE EDGE PLATE ▽
43 × 45 cm. Multifired glazes, slips
and enamels.
PHOTO BY KIND PERMISSION OF WINSTONE LTD

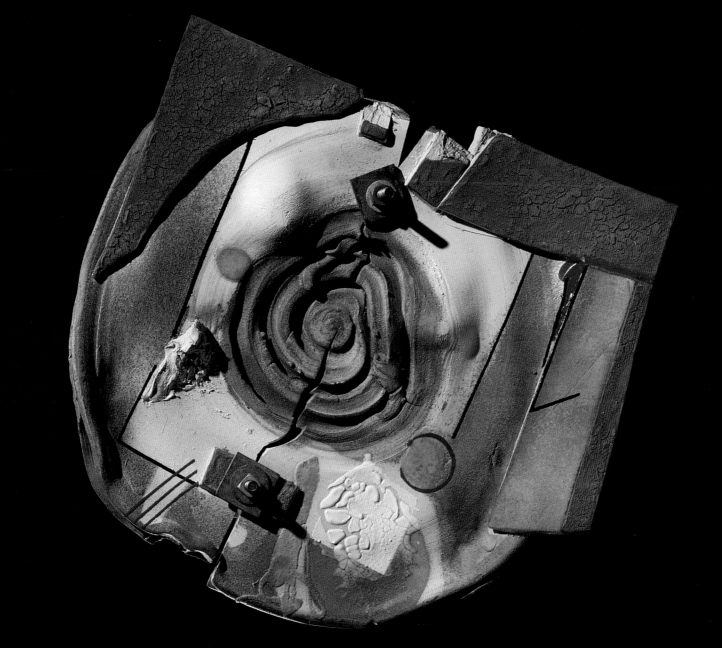

DAVID GRIFFITH

1

My first pots were made purely as functional works. My main production is still domestic ware, fired to 1280°C in two electric kilns. I work at home with my wife, Lynne, but she is devoting more time to photography than pottery now.

As my experience has increased, aesthetic appreciation has become more important. Lately I have derived much more pleasure from non-functional pieces which give visual enjoyment to me and to the people who buy them.

Recently I have been making raku pots with matt copper glazes. The variety of colour in these pieces is quite amazing and very satisfying.

1. and **2.** Assembling slab form
3. Carving out trinket box
PHOTOS — LYNNE GRIFFITH

2

3

BIOGRAPHY

1964 Began career behind an office desk
1974 Began to take interest in pottery equipment after wife Lynne started making pots; soon I was too. Live in suburban Nelson on a hillside overlooking Tahuna Beach and Tasman Bay, but commuted across town to Nelson's first workshop group, Craft Potters.
1976 Attended evening classes and potted in spare time
1977 Joined the steering committee to set up the city-based Community Potters Group Began career as a fulltime potter, making a range of domestic ware
1981 While Australian, Marc Sauvage, was working in Nelson, was introduced to strictly ordered geometric forms, with strong colour in the form of low-temperature commercial glazes Also introduced to direct and rapid hand-building techniques at a Len Castle demonstration in Nelson
1985 President, Nelson Potters Association

Exhibitions

1980 Nelson Potters Association annual exhibition
1981 NZ Society of Potters annual exhibition
1985 BNZ Art Award, NZ Academy of Fine Arts exhibition, Wellington
1985–6 Exhibited annually, Fletcher Brownbuilt Pottery Award, Auckland
1986 *Ceramics '86*, Govett-Brewster Art Gallery, New Plymouth

Collections

Forrester Gallery, Oamaru

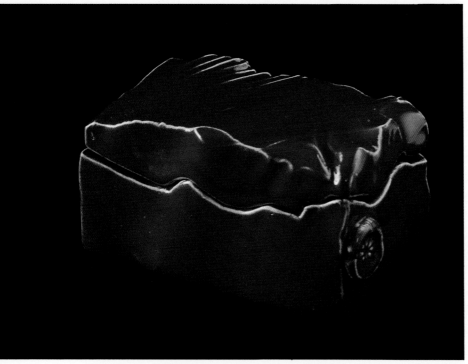

◁ TRINKET BOX, 1985
Length — 11 cm; width — 5 cm;
height — 5 cm. Carved from piece
of clay and hollowed out. White
stoneware body, bisqued to
1150°C, glost to 980°C.
Commercial glazes brushed on.
PHOTO — LYNNE GRIFFITH

PLATTER, WITH ADDITIONS, 1985 ▷
22 × 18 cm. Rolled slab with
handmade additions. White
stoneware body, bisqued to
1150°C, glost to 980°C.
Commercial glazes brushed on.
PHOTO — LYNNE GRIFFITH

◁ SLAB FORM, 1986
20 × 24 cm. Assembled from rolled
slabs. White stoneware body,
bisqued to 1150°C, glost to 980°C.
Commercial glazes brushed on.
PHOTO — LYNNE GRIFFITH

'THE SLIDE' —   ▷
RAKU POT, 1986
Height — 15 cm; width — 17 cm.
Raku fired with matt copper glaze.
PHOTO — LYNNE GRIFFITH

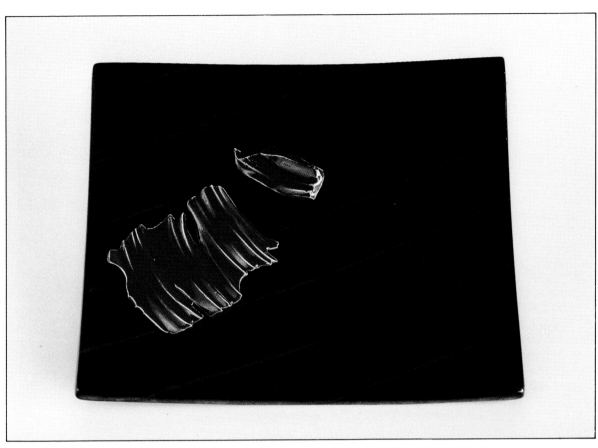

JEAN HASTEDT

I work in both stoneware and porcelain. All of my forms are functional and I now fire in a gas-fired downdraft kiln. Most of my work is wheel thrown: bowls, containers, teapots, etc. I also enjoy making slab boxes.

I strive to have my work visually simple and hope the glaze selected will complete the harmony. All my work is small. I love throwing and assembling teapots, finding the exercise a quietening creative experience. I do not make vast quantities of pieces, as each one demands a deal of time and care to bring it to the desired finish.

Glazing I love and I could spend forever testing — which I did in 1985 at a post-graduate year at Chisholm Institute of Technology in Melbourne.

My present interest lies with celadon glazes, blue in particular. Many of my new glazes call out for new forms, which I have not yet resolved, but they tend towards even more simple forms, leaving the glaze to stand alone.

I work alone in a medium-sized workshop on my quarter-acre property at Otaihanga, Paraparaumu. I am surrounded by silver birch trees and within walking distance is the Waikanae River, which I find very peaceful and sometimes inspirational for both potting and painting.

Celadon triaxial glaze test

Tested on Morlynn porcelain clay, PS 1000, and bisque fired to 960°C.

1 kg of the base glaze was prepared and ball milled for 4 hours. Three portions of 250 ml of the wet glaze were then set aside, the specific gravity determined and the dry glaze ingredients contained in 250 ml of glaze calculated, using Brongniart's formula. The red iron and talc were added to the remaining 2 x 250 ml of glaze, which was then mortar-and-pestle blended for 10 minutes.

The three glazes were then blended volumetrically and applied to the tile: four of the tiles were made and fired in light, medium and heavy reduction and oxidation to 1280°C. (See over.)

1. Fluting porcelain jars   2. Weighing up test glazes
3. Throwing porcelain jars
PHOTOS — JOHN CHEESE

Base glaze (A)

K_2O	.21
Na_2O	.06
Al_2O_3	.6
SiO_2	3.10
MgO	.26
CaO	.47

Base glaze (B)
Base glaze (A) plus 2.5% red iron

Base glaze (C)
Base glaze (A) plus 5% talc

2

3

BIOGRAPHY
Has a background as a cartographer and
graphic artist
1974 Apprentice potter to Yvonne Rust
1975 Built studio and double-chambered
oil-fired kiln at Otaihanga, Paraparaumu
1982 Purchased 9 cu. ft. gas kiln with a QEII
Arts Council grant
1985 Post-graduate study, Chisholm Institute
of Technology, Melbourne

Exhibitions
1974– Exhibiting member, NZ Society of
Potters
Several solo and joint exhibitions in London,
Canada and Australia
1979– Exhibited annually, Fletcher Brownbuilt
Pottery Award, Auckland
1981 *The Bowl*, Crafts Council of NZ
exhibition, Wellington
Artist member, NZ Academy of Fine Arts,
Wellington
1982 BNZ Art Award, NZ Academy of Fine Arts
exhibition, Wellington
1983 Selected by NZ Society of Potters to
submit work for 41st Concorso Internazionalle
della Ceramica d'Arte, Faenza, Italy
The Great NZ Box Show, Crafts Council of NZ,
Wellington City Art Gallery
1984 Guest potter, Christchurch Arts Festival
Double Exposure, Crafts Council of NZ
paintings and glass kaleidoscopes exhibition,
Wellington.
Clay and Watercolour, Wellington City Gallery
ANZ Bank exhibition, Melbourne
Westpac Gallery, Victoria Arts Centre,
Melbourne
Women in Art, Chisholm Institute of
Technology, Melbourne
1986 *Continuity and Change*, Jiangsu
Province, China

Awards
1980 Merit Award Winner, Fletcher Brownbuilt
Pottery Award, Auckland
1982 Winner, BNZ Art Award, Academy of Fine
Arts exhibition, Wellington

Collections
Hawkes Bay Art Gallery and Museum, Napier
Suter Art Gallery, Nelson
Auckland Studio Potters
Dowse Art Gallery, Lower Hutt
Auckland Institute and Museum
Chisholm Institute of Technology, Melbourne

◁ BOWL
Height — 10 cm; width — 13 cm.
Porcelain, celadon glaze.
PHOTO — JOHN CHEESE

TRIAXIAL GLAZE TEST ▷
Celadon. Research done at
Chisholm Institute of Technology,
Melbourne
PHOTO — JOHN CHEESE

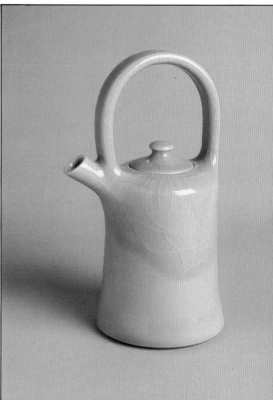

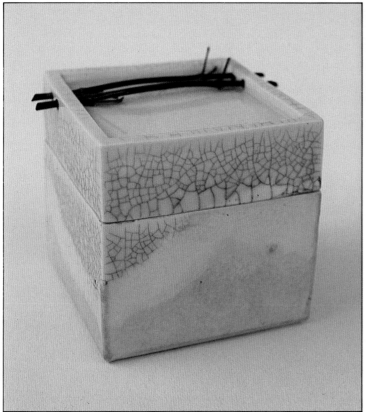

TEAPOT △
Height — 20 cm; width — 12 cm.
Thrown. Porcelain, celadon glaze.
PHOTO — JOHN CHEESE

◁ BOX WITH BAMBOO TRIM
Height — 11 cm; width — 11 cm.
Porcelain, with crackle and barium
glaze.
PHOTO — JOHN CHEESE

SET OF THREE SLAB BOXES ▷
Heights — 8 cm, 7 cm, 6 cm; widths
— 9 cm, 8 cm, 7 cm. Porcelain,
celadon glaze.
PHOTO — JOHN CHEESE

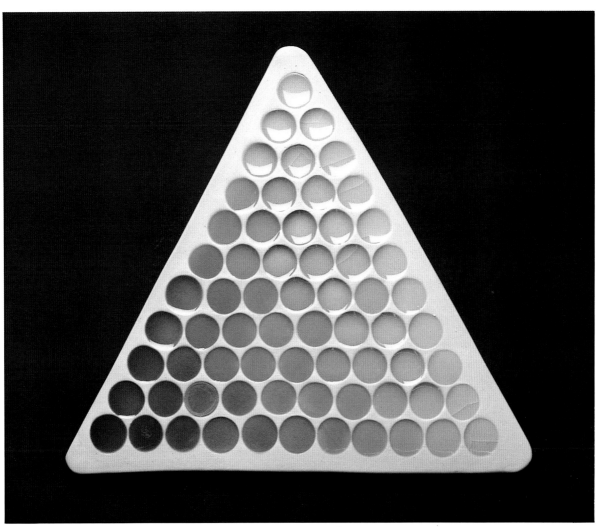

CAMPBELL HEGAN

work in two distinctly different modes. Much of the work that I produce is utilitarian and, with the exception of the teapots, the forms are simple and uncluttered. They develop and change over long periods of work, often without my noticing.

Although I don't consciously bring any influences to this work, despite myself the references to Japanese and Korean pots are clear. I do try to imbue my throwing with the vitality and freshness that is the essence of those traditions. The spirit of the works that come from these traditions is the natural outcome of the personal philosophies of their makers. Much that is contained in those philosophies is important to me also. The way I choose to work is a reflection of aspects of that. The objects that I make reflect how I think and how I am.

I enjoy making things unselfconsciously for everyday use. The more I enjoy it, the easier it gets; the easier it gets, the more I enjoy it . . . . The rest of my work is very

BIOGRAPHY
Born 1946
1965–6 Fulltime professional actor
1966–71 Involved in NZ television production
1972 First studio and kiln, Waiatarua, Auckland
1979 Set up present studio with Andrea Barrett, Devonport
1981 Wrote and presented a series of six programmes on ceramics in NZ (historical, traditions, contemporary)
1981–3 Wrote and presented programmes (including reviews and critiques) on the annual Fletcher Brownbuilt Pottery Awards
1983 Wrote and presented a series of four programmes on contemporary ceramics in New Zealand
1983–4 Vice-President, NZ Crafts Council
1984–5 President, NZ Crafts Council
1984 Wrote and presented programme on Fletcher Brownbuilt Pottery Award (with Don Reitz from USA)
1985 Appointed to NZ Crafts Education Advisory Committee
1985 Wrote and presented programme on Fletcher Brownbuilt Pottery Award (with Maria Kuczcynska, Poland)
1986 Selected and curated two large ceramics and glass shows, *Out of New Zealand 1* and *Out of New Zealand 2*, for exhibition in the USA. Has selected a number of regional and national ceramic exhibitions in New Zealand over the years.

Exhibitions
1978– Exhibited annually, Fletcher Brownbuilt Pottery Award, Auckland
1980 Antipodes Gallery, Wellington
1981 McMurray Gallery, Palmerston North
Alicat Gallery, Auckland
1984 Compendium Gallery, Auckland
McMurray Gallery, Palmerston North
Blackfriars Gallery, Sydney
Young Masters Gallery, Brisbane
Clay and Glass Az Art, Flagstaff, Arizona, USA
1985 Solander Gallery, Canberra
CSA Gallery, Christchurch
Crafts Council of Australia exhibition, Sydney
Rotary International art competition
1986 Elizabeth Fortner Gallery, Santa Barbara, Calif.
International Gallery, San Diego, Calif.

Awards
1978 Merit Award winner, Fletcher Brownbuilt Pottery Award, Auckland
1985 Premier Award winner, Rotary International art competition
Merit Award winner, Fletcher Brownbuilt Pottery Award, Auckland

Collections
Mingei Museum, Japan
Auckland Institute and Museum
Robert McDougall Gallery, Christchurch
Presidential collection, Jakarta, Indonesia
NZ Embassies in Washington, Paris and Peking

selfconscious and calculated. The forms are thrown and altered and added to. They are vehicles for me to explore ideas about form and space, tension and balance. In many of these pieces I utilise the concept of the vessel for ritual or ceremony. These seemed a natural development of my utilitarian objects and vessels, and allow endless scope for exploration and abstraction.

I work with earthenware, stoneware and porcelain. The earthenware is unglazed and sparsely decorated with dry engobes. It is gas fired with very slight reduction to 1100°C.

The stoneware and porcelain is gas fired to 1320°C in reduction. Although the risks of losing work are greatly increased, I prefer to fire these pots at cone 12 instead of the more usual cone 9 or 10 so as to achieve the greater depth of glaze, only possible at these higher temperatures. Greater integration of clay and glaze is also made possible in this way.

RITUAL VESSEL
Height — 26 cm. Stoneware
PHOTO — CAMPBELL HEGAN

TEAPOTS △
Heights — 29 cm, 23 cm, 17 cm.
Shino glaze.
PHOTO — CAMPBELL HEGAN

OVOID ▽
30 × 30 cm. Copper-red glaze.
PHOTO — CAMPBELL HEGAN

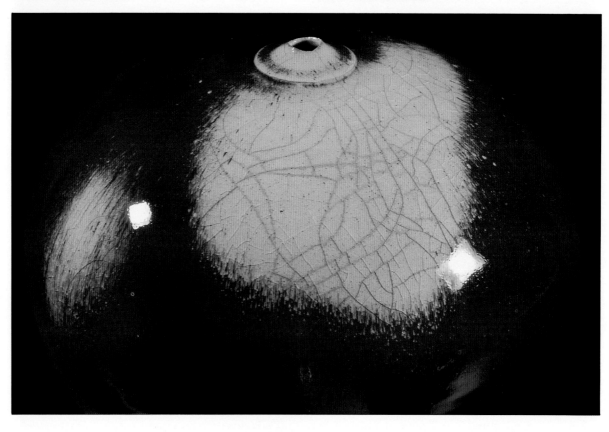

BLOSSOM POT △
36 × 34 cm. Copper-red glaze.

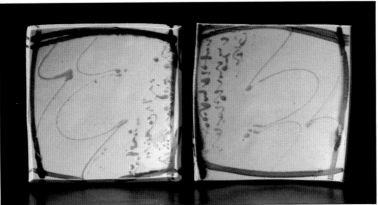

◁ DISHES
18 × 18 cm. Slip-trailed porcelain.

ALAN KESTLE

I work almost entirely with two forms, the bowl and the bottle — forms which hold endless challenges for me. The shapes of the pieces need not be complex. Simple, well balanced forms that 'stand on their own' before glazing or decorating, are often the most successful finished pieces.

I use porcelain clay for various reasons:
— it affords a neutral background which does not react with glazes or detract from any subsequent decoration;
— it gives a striking contrast when left exposed on the rims and edges of finished forms;
— the fine texture of the clay allows me to produce smooth, burnished surfaces, essential for fine inlaying.

I have deliberately restricted the zone of ceramics I work in. This specialisation gives me a definite focus on which I can concentrate and try to perfect my work.

At present I live in Titirangi, Auckland, and work in a studio adjoining the house.

I use Podmore's porcelain and make predominantly decorative pieces glazed in black and white or burnished smooth, unglazed, with inlaid black lines. Most recent work is with on-glaze enamels, applied by airbrush, to accent rims and edges.

All work is electric-kiln fired to 1240°C.

PHOTO — CES THOMAS

BIOGRAPHY
1948 Born Auckland
Qualified structural draughtsman — still in practising partnership
1976 Attended pottery classes at Auckland Studio Potters Centre — tutor John Parker
1978 Began potting professionally part-time
1979—80 Layout designer for the Auckland Studio Potters annual exhibition, Auckland Institute and Museum
1979—85 Member, 12 Potters Cooperative, Auckland
1982 Began potting fulltime

Exhibitions
1979—81 Exhibited annually, Fletcher Brownbuilt Pottery Award, Auckland
1981 Three-man show, Media Gallery, Wellington
1982 Media Gallery, Wellington
1984—6 Exhibited annually, Fletcher Brownbuilt Pottery Award, Auckland
1984 Two-man show, Media Gallery, Wellington
Clay and Glass Az Art, Flagstaff, Arizona, USA
1985 New Vision Ceramic Arts, Auckland
1986 Compendium Gallery, Auckland
Elizabeth Fortner Gallery, Santa Barbara, Calif.

Collections
Auckland Institute and Museum
Suter Art Gallery, Nelson

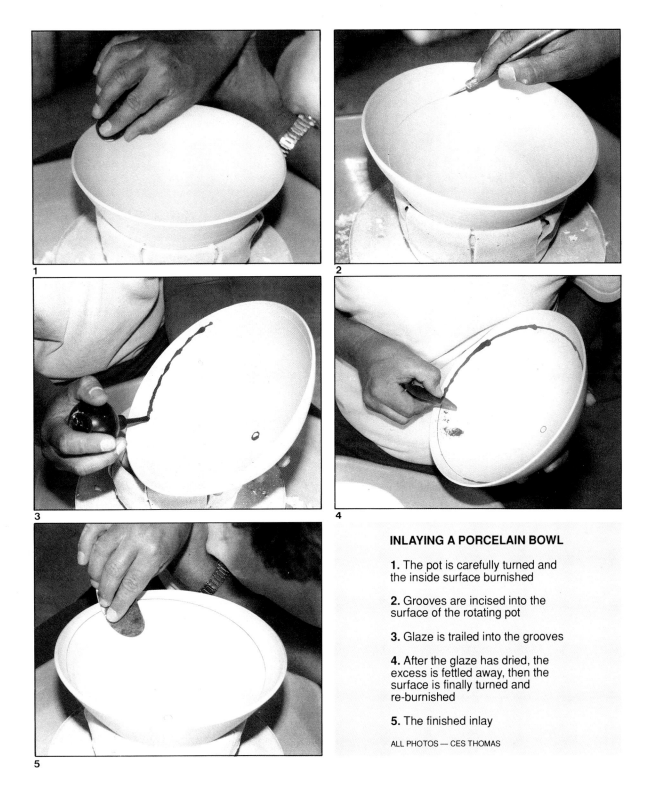

INLAYING A PORCELAIN BOWL

1. The pot is carefully turned and the inside surface burnished

2. Grooves are incised into the surface of the rotating pot

3. Glaze is trailed into the grooves

4. After the glaze has dried, the excess is fettled away, then the surface is finally turned and re-burnished

5. The finished inlay

ALL PHOTOS — CES THOMAS

PORCELAIN BOTTLES △
Black glaze lines inlaid into
burnished surface
PHOTO — CES THOMAS

PORCELAIN BOWL ▽
Width — 15 cm. Gloss black glaze,
gold lustre rim.
PHOTO — CES THOMAS

PORCELAIN BOWL ▷
Width — 25 cm. Matt black glaze
with on-glazed rim.
PHOTO — CES THOMAS

PORCELAIN BOWL ▷
Width — 32 cm. Gloss black glaze
outside; black glaze lines inlaid into
burnished inner surface
PHOTO — CES THOMAS

LEO KING

Over the last few years some of my work has been based upon forms which owe their existence to the balance of natural forces such as the sphere and of which the soap bubble is a good example. I have spent some time exploring the ways in which the latter may be manipulated and I am impressed by the diversity of its architectural application. However, as a form I find it self-contained, internally focussed and in many ways unacceptably dominant.

The vertical columnar form or pillar which is the subject of my current work seems to have more freedom. While it obeys the laws of other forces, it gives the impression of seeking to resist them and it is easy to associate this with the illusion of creativity and growth. Its capacity to act as a sign or symbol has been exploited in the human context where it may refer, for instance, to ambition, or express some religious perception. Like the sphere, it is a timeless form and has been diversely treated by

SLIP CASTING

Slip casting is an easy and accurate method of reproducing simple forms in clay. The method of forming, which is dependent upon the chemically increased fluidity of the clay body and the absorbency of plaster, made it a natural choice for certain industrial processes. I have chosen to use it because of its simplicity, accuracy and speed and because I have a requirement for the replication of thin-walled basic shapes which are the prerequisite of my work.

I use the standard method and materials for the deflocculation of the clay body and although this is predominantly sodium silicate, I find that the addition of a small percentage of soda ash improves the handling characteristics of the casting.

For a number of years I have used an imported white body which is ultimately fired to 1240°C in an oxidising atmosphere in an electric kiln.

My approach to moulds with particular relation to columnar forms is modular and therefore necessitates the use of mechanical methods of retention. I use an ordinary casting plaster which is prepared to give a 1:1.3 or 130 mix, giving an absorbency of about 40 per cent and which is considered optimum for a casting mould.

Example

Calculated mould volume 1000 ccs

$$\frac{1000 \times 5}{7} = 714 \text{ ccs volume of water}$$

$714 \times 1.3 = 928$ g weight of plaster

artists, architects and designers, from a fundamental unit of Greek architecture to its use as subject matter by Abstract Expressionist painters such as Newman or Pollock.

Overlaying my interest in these basic forms is an appreciation of geometry, the rules of which apply constraints to a form but at the same time impart to it a unique elegance and simplicity. This is supported and emphasised by working in black and white which makes a definitive statement uncompromised by intermediate shades of grey or by colour. However, colour, when used in this context and in a controlled and limited manner, is allowed to make a pungent and dramatic impact.

For similar reasons, the textural capabilities of the material are suppressed in order that the ideas expressed upon the various surfaces of the work, graphically or by low relief, may be projected with more intensity.

The linear form of the column, which can

1. and **2.** The assembly of the mould

3. The assembly of the mould into the holding jig

4. Filling with slip. Care needs to be taken when filling deep moulds, to pour at a uniform speed and to keep the stream of liquid clay as close to the centre of the mould as possible. If the clay is allowed to splash on the surface of the mould still exposed, imperfections in the surface of the cast will obviously result.

5. A hoist is useful to assist in the raising of large volumes of slip and in accurate pouring. I use the same device to lift the filled mould and to control the pouring out of the unrequired slip upon the completion of the casting process.

Dependent upon the ambient conditions, I generally seal the mould and leave overnight in order that the cast may achieve a state of dryness sufficient to make it self-supporting but at the same time suitable for subsequent operations.

6. Separation of the mould.

7. and **8.** Trimming off the top of the cast. A ground down hacksaw blade is a useful tool.

ALL PHOTOS — CES THOMAS

have a wide dimensional variability, makes its spatial relationship to similar forms more demanding and perhaps more interesting than combinations of other forms which possess a different configuration. In combination, however, with these different forms the column can be visually very stimulating.

The pieces which I currently make I perceive as maquettes for sculptural forms which I am at present unable to achieve but which are able to exist in their own right in a range of environments. They are contemporary in so far as they reflect the elements of precision or accuracy which is symbolic of the technology of the last few decades and therefore, in part, fulfil the purpose and function of any art form. They are, however, also made in accordance with principles which have been fundamental in our human development and consequently reflect the paradox apparent in the rigid formality of the architecture of many natural forms.

Each piece of work illustrated opposite has a white porcellaneous body and was fired at 1240°C.

BIOGRAPHY

Born in the UK. Worked in Aerospace and missile systems. BA in Art History, Auckland University. Training in sculpture and ceramics, St Albans School of Art, Herts, UK.
1971 Emigrated to NZ
1972–5 Secretary, Auckland Studio Potters
1976 Director, Auckland Studio Potters Centre, Onehunga
1978–81 President, NZ Society of Potters
1980 Artist member, NZ Academy of Fine Arts, Wellington

Exhibitions
1972–6 Auckland Studio Potters annual exhibitions
1976–85 NZ Society of Potters annual exhibitions
1977 Alicat Gallery, Auckland, with Jim Greig
Pottery and Greenstone, CSA Gallery, Christchurch with Donn Salt
1977–85 Exhibited annually, Fletcher Brownbuilt Pottery Award, Auckland
1978 Albany Village Pottery
NZ Ministry of Foreign Affairs Collection, Royal Museum, Brussels, The Hague and London
Antipodes Gallery, Wellington, with Koroko Weavers
1979 37th Concorso Internazionalle della Ceramica d'Arte, Faenza, Italy
1980–5 IBM, Caltex, Williams and BNZ award exhibitions, Wellington
1981 39th Concorso Internazionalle della Ceramica d'Arte, Faenza, Italy
The Bowl, Crafts Council of NZ exhibition, Wellington City Art Gallery

1983 *The Bowl*, Asian Zone of the World Crafts Council exhibition, touring to India, Pakistan, Thailand and Fiji
Gallery 242, Hastings
Compendium Gallery, Auckland
41st Concorso Internazionalle della Ceramica d'Arte, Faenza, Italy
1984 Centre Gallery, Hamilton
Clay and Glass Az Art, Flagstaff, Arizona, USA
1985 The Pottery and Friends Gallery, Christchurch, with Roger Brittain
Craft and Architecture, BNZ award exhibition, Auckland Institute and Museum

Awards
1981 Merit Award winner, Fletcher Brownbuilt Pottery Award, Auckland
1982 ICI Bursary for Sculpture and Painting
1984 Merit Award winner, Fletcher Brownbuilt Pottery Award, Auckland
1985 Merit Award winner, Fletcher Brownbuilt Pottery Award, Auckland

Collections
Royal Museum, Glasgow
Perth Technical Institute, Western Australia
Private collections, Germany, USA, Japan, Australia and England
National Museum, Wellington
Auckland Institute and Museum
Robert McDougall Gallery, Christchurch
Suter Gallery, Nelson
Hastings City Cultural Centre Gallery
Hawkes Bay Art Gallery and Museum, Napier
Rotorua City Council
Fletcher Brownbuilt collection in Auckland and Wellington

Publications
Craft New Zealand, Blumhardt and Brake, Wellington 1981
International Contemporary Ceramics, Storr Britz, Germany, 1980
Studio Ceramics, Peter Lane, England, 1983

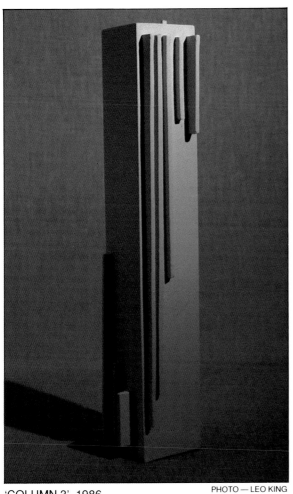

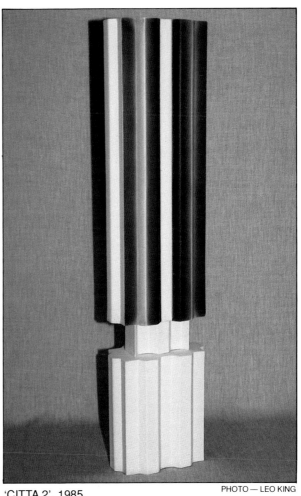

'COLUMN 3', 1986
PHOTO — LEO KING
Height — 49 cm; length — 13 cm; width — 10 cm.
White unglazed body. Cast and assembled.

'CITTA 2', 1985
PHOTO — LEO KING
Height — 74 cm; length — 17 cm; width — 11 cm.
White unglazed body, oxide sprayed decor.

TABLE SCULPTURE, 1985   Height — 13 cm; length — 54 cm; width — 9 cm.   Unglazed white body, black oxide. ▽

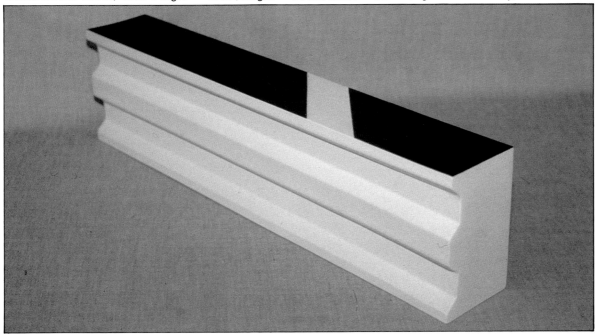

PETER LANGE

I wandered into potting by a series of accidents in 1973. Did ceramic country service until 1978 near Warkworth: diesel kiln, cone 10 stoneware, middle-of-the-road domestics.

My main influences have been the marketplace, Crown Lynn, function.

Probably I have derived more satisfaction out of making a living, running a business, producing repetitive functional ware, than out of any particular pot.

Have made an occasional detour into the less functional, usually by the way of the humorous. Very little influence from the Oriental ethic; in fact an almost deliberate avoidance of the tasteful. After

1. A visit by Richard Shaw from San Francisco,
2. A trip to the West Coast of USA,
3. A grant from QEII Arts Council,

I developed a more sculptural style. One of my pieces with neon and slip casting won a Merit Award in the Fletcher Brownbuilt Exhibition. Eventually to the super-realistic fakery of Richard Shaw — slip casting, a lot of technical problems overcome and still to be overcome.

A deliberate avoidance of the elemental. Mostly surface treatment, humorous or satirical approach, perhaps a tendency to 'ceramic one-liners'.

Most recently a grudging acceptance of the effects of flame on clay — still slip casting realistic elements but using terracotta and wood-filled saggars, developing architectural forms.

Been up many aesthetic cul-de-sacs. Travelled a fairly haphazard path through the ceramic mirror maze. Now more inclined to accept bits of a lot of techniques and apply them to the creative notions that arise in a relatively random way, depending on day-to-day influences — weather, politics, money — hopefully avoiding the pretentious and flirting with the absurd.

The work illustrated is slip-cast earthenware, fired at 1140°C, with decals, lustres and on-glazes at 740—750°C. Elements are cast separately and slipped together before firing. Moulds are made from found objects and are up to eight pieces, depending on whether I have to break them to get the object out.

BIOGRAPHY

1944 Born Otahuhu, Auckland
Educated at Otahuhu College
Architectural school for two years before dropping out
1963–73 Wandered around. Worked in freezing works, factories, building sites, boat building and prospecting. Travelled. Cleaned silver at Buckingham Palace. Drove a London cab for a year.
1968 Married
1973 Returned to New Zealand to live in the country at Bombay, a mile from Lex Dawson. Inevitably got caught up in the bonanza of the mid 70s making inadequate pots for adequate money
1974 Moved to Warkworth, doing my country service for five years with a diesel kiln
1975 Joined Albany Village Pottery. Pots improved. Raised three kids with my wife, Ro.
1979 Moved into Mt Eden and set up The Potter's Arms as a workshop, retail outlet and home
1981 Bought a nearby house and converted The Potter's Arms into a workshop-retail cooperative, which served as a social and political meeting-place for a lot of Mt Eden artists and craftspeople
Richard Shaw came as the Fletcher Brownbuilt judge this year. His approach to clay delighted me and has influenced me ever since. (Other influences:
Spike Milligan — lateral thinker;
Westfield Freezing Works — hard work;
Crown Lynn — especially those handpainted fruit cups and saucers — my tradition;
The Times crossword)

Exhibitions
1981 Exhibitor, Fletcher Brownbuilt Pottery Award, Auckland
1982– Auckland Studio Potters annual exhibitions
1984– Exhibited annually, Fletcher Brownbuilt Pottery Award, Auckland
Clay and Glass Az Art, Flagstaff, Arizona, USA

Awards
1984 Merit Award winner, Fletcher Brownbuilt Pottery Award, Auckland
1986 Merit Award winner, Fletcher Brownbuilt Pottery Award, Auckland

Collections
Work is represented in The Beehive, Wellington

PHOTO — ANNA CAMPBELL

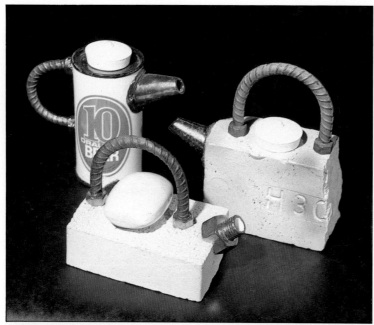

◁ THREE TEAPOTS
Life-size
PHOTO — HOWARD WILLIAMS

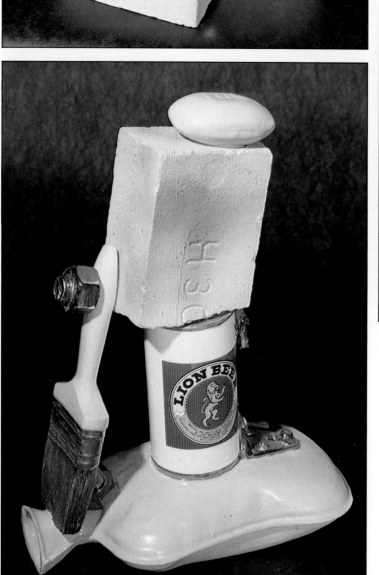

BEDSIDE LAMP △
Height — 40 cm
PHOTO — HOWARD WILLIAMS

◁ LIDDED JAR
Height — 20 cm
PHOTO — HOWARD WILLIAMS

TARANAKI BEDSIDE LAMP ▷
Height — 30 cm
PHOTO — HOWARD WILLIAMS

PATTI MEADS

Viewing the exquisite fourteenth, fifteenth and sixteenth century lustres in the Louvre, in Paris, six years ago made me feel I should leave lustres entirely alone. Originally I used them for creating rivers, moonlit skies, waters and so forth, in large ceramic murals. Knowing that I hadn't a hope of doing anything like those magnificent old pieces, I still felt a longing to produce something which, although entirely different, would at least give me a chance to use lustres in a wider and more varied way than I had previously. I wanted to use them as a total decoration.

Slowly I evolved my own techniques, by reading widely, taking up any promising idea and, by trial and error, making it work for me.

Basically mine is a lustre-on-lustre technique (using commercial lustres) which is spread and broken by the use of an oil medium. I have found that different grades of gold lustres give me different tones; for instance, one will give a bright gold, another a copper colour. On a clear or white glaze on porcelain, the thinner golds fire to rose pink, or lavender, depending on the base glaze being used, while on a black glaze the thinner gold is a rich copper through to

1. Undercutting the base of a slab-built skinny bottle to give it more lift.

2. Working on a centripetal form. Such pieces are made using two moulds — a large half-sphere and a shallow curve. When firm enough to handle, they are joined with the top resting in a curved shape while the bottom is first paddled firmly on to it and then the edges are refined with a steel rib before being burnished when leather hard.

3. Spraying an unglazed tile, which has been bisqued to 1020°C, with a solution of iron sulphate before smoking it in wood shavings.

PHOTOS — SAL CRISCILLO

bronze. Exploring these variations is still something of a learning process.

I use an electric kiln and until the middle of 1985 I worked entirely with glazed surfaces, using a low fired porcelain which is translucent at 1220°C, with subsequent lustre firings of gold and platinum at 750°C. The richness of the lustres demands simple forms, to complement the extravagance of the patterning. I use both thrown and hand-moulded forms, one of my favourites being an egg shape which lends itself perfectly to lustre decoration. Large plates are a wonderful base for experimenting with patterns of gold and platinum.

In 1985 I began to explore the effects of smoke on porcelain, and this has led me into a new field. I burnish the pieces when leather hard, using stones or spoons depending on the contours, before firing them in the electric kiln to between 980°C —1020°C (the form dictating the temperature). Gold and platinum lustres are then applied before firing to 750°C. (Often two or three applications may be necessary to achieve the results I require, with consequent refirings.)

The final stage is to place the works in sawdust in a collection of rubbish tins with holes drilled 15 cm from the base to allow air intake. The sawdust, which is ignited by using crumpled newspaper, burns slowly, carbonising the clay and altering the lustres. The use of treated sawdust from commercial timber merchants and the incorporation, when available, of aluminium filings can cause the results to be quite dramatic.

Late in 1986 I began using iron and copper sulphate on the pots which were going to be smoked. I discovered that the use of shavings rather than sawdust gives more heat and I have areas of reduction and oxidation occurring, giving the soluble salts incredible overtones.

I'm continuing to experiment with these but have also begun using fine sprays of low coloured glazes instead of the metal lustres, before smoking in shavings, and the results are very promising so far.

I have been fortunate over the years to have my work commissioned by Foreign Affairs for our chanceries and embassies throughout the world and to have special purchases made for gifts which our diplomats, the Prime Minister and Members of Parliament give to visiting dignitaries and members of the Royal Family, and to Heads of State when on overseas visits.

Because of the way I work, the results are never totally predictable and change is absolutely inevitable and that's what I love. Everything I read, everything I strive to achieve, makes my results different from the last time. The day is always too short, the firing could always be better, and tomorrow just might bring what one hopes for — that's pottery for me, an endless striving and a will to achieve.

BIOGRAPHY

1968 Began potting at the Wellington High School evening institute under tutor Ian McClymont
1970 Taught for the final term
Attended advanced classes, University Extension Summer School; tutor Evelyn Hastings
1970–3 Vice-president, Wellington Potters Association
1972 Gained juried membership, NZ Society of Potters
Artist member, NZ Academy of Fine Arts
1973–7 President, Wellington Potters Association
1979–80 Wellington delegate to NZ Society of Potters

Exhibitions
1982 40th Concorso Internazionalle della Ceramica d'Arte, Faenza, Italy
1986 44th Concorso Internazionalle della Ceramica d'Arte, Faenza, Italy

Awards
1979 Lombard Art Award for high attainment in pottery, NZ Academy of Fine Arts, Wellington

Collections
New Zealand House, London
Modern Art Museum, Manila, Philippines
Power House Museum, Sydney
Private collections in New Zealand and overseas

BOTTLE, 1979 ▷
10 × 8 cm. Black glazed porcelain with gold
and platinum lustres.
PHOTO — SAL CRISCILLO

BOTTLE AND BOXES, 1984 △
Bottle, wheel-thrown — 15 × 9 cm; oval box,
handbuilt — 11 × 9 cm; box, wheel-thrown —
5 × 8 cm.
Black mirror glaze on porcelain with gold
and platinum lustres.
PHOTO — SAL CRISCILLO

CENTRIPETAL FORM, 1986 ▷
34 × 42 cm. Hand-moulded forms joined,
burnished and fired to 1020˚C. Lustred with
gold and platinum, refired to 750 ˚C.
Smoked in sawdust containing aluminium
filings.
PHOTO — MICHAEL OVEREND

MARGARET MILNE

I find it hard to be articulate about my feeling for clay — it has given me so much. I am deeply conscious of the change that working as a potter and with potters has brought to my outlook and to my sense of values. I feel a greater care and appreciation of our environment and the resources and materials which are there for our use and continuing discovery.

I feel a greater joy with success and an easier acceptance of disappointment, but most of all I believe that creative thought and action are important for everyone in whatever direction their abilities lie. Clay, with its infinite moods, leads us on an eventful and fulfilling journey.

For inlaid work I use body stains to colour David Leach porcelain. Many colours are mixed, usually 10 gm stain to 200 gm body. This gives a strong colour and can be modified by adding differing amounts of the white porcelain clay.

The inlay patterns are made by putting flat, rolled-out sections of different colours on top of each other. These are either sliced into strips or rolled up firmly and then sliced to form patterns. Sometimes pieces are joined to form continuous strips and sometimes they are used singly.

Bowls and boxes have areas cut out and the inlay inserted when the piece is leather hard, pressed firmly and turned later to give a sharp, clear pattern. They are polished but unglazed. The same process is used for the picture pieces which are rolled out flat. Coloured clays are then inserted into the already cut-out pattern, rolled firmly again and then eased into a mould and dried slowly.

All work is fired to Orton cone 9 in an electric kiln.

BIOGRAPHY
1958 Interest in pottery began with classes at night school. No formal art training.
1967 Travelled to Japan and spent some months living and working in a Japanese pottery.
1969 Set up a cottage workshop with diesel and electric kilns for working and teaching. In time this developed into a type of cooperative workshop.
1973 Travelled in UK and when visiting potters became particularly interested in those working in porcelain
1974 Visited People's Republic of China, Japan and South Korea as a member of a cultural delegation of five potters, sponsored by the NZ Ministry of Foreign Affairs
1978 Visited potters in UK and Scandanavia
1980 Attended World Crafts Council Conference in Vienna

Exhibitions
Exhibited in group shows: Victoria and Albert Museum, London; Brussels; USA; Japan; Australia and New Zealand

Collections
Represented in museum, gallery and private collections in New Zealand and overseas

PHOTO — HARU SAMESHIMA

BOTTLE AND TWO AGATE POTS △
PHOTO — HARU SAMESHIMA

PICTURE PLATTER ▽
PHOTO — HARU SAMESHIMA

BOWL AND LIDDED BOX ▷
Bowl — 20 cm diameter; box —
8 cm diameter. Inlaid patterns.
PHOTO — HARU SAMESHIMA

CHESTER NEALIE

During my early years of salt glazing I became enraptured by the subtle qualities that exists under the pots and between the bricks of my kiln. In 1978 I was invited to lecture at the World Craft Council Conference in Kyoto. This Japanese experience enabled me to have a close look at the cross-draught tunnel kilns in Tajimi and Shigaraki.

I decided to construct an anagama-type tunnel kiln but incorporate a more efficient firebox that would produce a maximum amount of ash deposit on the pots. Over the last six years I have gradually increased the time of firing so that a comparison could be established.

1. Workshop **2.** Seven-metre anagama kiln
3. Side stoking the kiln
PHOTO 1 — CHESTER NEALIE; 2 AND 3, HILARY NEALIE

An anagama firing

I thought I'd give here an insight into my present potting cycle. It usually begins four to five months before the first day of firing, when the clay is mixed and the wood is delivered and stacked. I use pine slabs rejected from a local mill, all cut to about 1 metre in length. Approximately 10 tonnes are stacked around the kiln and allowed to dry.

The next three months are spent making the clay shapes that are compatible with my sense of aesthetic freedom, as well as having a form and texture on which the flames can create their own individual, magical patterns. This love of raw clay is the essence of woodfiring. Every touch, every sign, every emotion is revealed in the clay. You can't be false. All is revealed, and

those skilled with eyes and heart can read your handling as in any novel. So to become one with your clay, the very wheel, tools, hands and heart must flow from within so that finally we are left with this mysterious object, full of subtleties of making and formed with the thought of fire heightening its joy still further. I often make pieces for a specific place in the kiln. This partly establishes the form and the clay. In one firing there may be five different types of clay and even more special kiln areas where a unique result will occur. Hence the making and the fire are mentally united from the beginning.

Three months' potting usually produces enough pieces from large to small. The kiln is 'de-ratted' prior to loading and the floor re-covered with coarse silica sand. As the floor bricks are laid directly on the ground, dampness can create steam cracks in the larger pots during firing, so broken shells from the ancient Maori midden nearby support the bases or sides. Great care is taken in loading. Touching pots are wadded with fire-clay or straw. All the time consideration is given to the passage of flame, especially through the bottom of the jumbled stacks of pots. As the palette of flame is infinite, you are creating colour patterns in the placement of each pot.

After four or five days of loading, the first day of firing is sheer bliss. At this time I use a local hardwood, manuka: unsplit, slow burning, short flame, aromatic and restful. A time to be alone, to become united again with the kiln. The kiln is damped down to steam dry the pots. Hourly stoking through

BIOGRAPHY
1942 Born Rotorua
1964 Began potting. Self-taught.
1966–71 Employed as science teacher
1972–5 Lecturer in ceramics at North Shore Teachers College, Auckland
1978 Lectured in ceramics at World Crafts Council Conference, Kyoto, Japan
1983 and 1986 Travelled to Australia. Judged Cairns Ceramic Exhibition and Caltex Invitation Exhibition, Townsville, and gave lectures throughout Queensland.
1987 Lives in a small coastal rural community on the Kaipara Harbour, Northland

Exhibitions
Has participated in numerous group exhibitions in New Zealand, Australia, Europe, Japan, Korea, China, the USA and Canada. Has held a number of solo exhibitions in New Zealand.

Awards
1982 Winner, Fletcher Brownbuilt Pottery Award, Auckland
1985 Winner, NZ Academy of Fine Arts BNZ Award, Wellington

The pots shown here were all fired for 5 days in an anagama kiln using 10 tonnes of wood
ALL PHOTOS — CES THOMAS

TWO POTS
Covered with ochre, these pots were both fired on the side of the anagama kiln below the stoke hole

WOODFIRED POT ▷
The marks shown are made from the piece lying on shells within the anagama kiln
PHOTO — CES THOMAS

the night enables your energy level to be conserved before the hectic final days. On the second day I gradually change to pine slabs, steadily increasing the volume of wood until 900°C is reached in the front. From now on the secondary air, sucking through the wood, is reduced; primary air, coming through the embers, is increased. All the time a steady rhythm is established to the tune the kiln dictates. The relationship of myself to the flame is the same sensuous serenity as exists when handling the clay.

Side stoking begins when the required temperature at that opening has been reached. This in turn heats the next area, and so stoking proceeds up the kiln. Meanwhile the front firebox is still being fed, alternating with side stoking. Many variables can exist at this stage: repetition of side stoking, amount of charcoal buildup, different types of wood, damper placement, kiln helpers, tiredness, euphoria. The unpredictability of the results never ceases to amaze.

The unknown variable to me is the firing down — the cooling, how fast, how slow. Sometimes a large log is fed in every while. The side-stoke embers continue to burn for days. The flames at this stage are superb, particularly the sodium flame if mangrove wood is used in selected spaces. It's so peaceful you feel as though you wish to bathe with the flames.

JOHN PARKER

PHOTO — MARIE BRITTAIN

I have always made things, but not always pots. Being an only child, I learnt to be resourceful. My childhood passions were for puppets, playhouse museum exhibits, chemistry sets and then as a magician. Pottery came quite by accident. During a very unhappy time struggling with maths, chemistry and physics for a B.Sc., I kept a friend company in a pottery night-school class.

I have been favoured by meeting some very special people at important formative times in my life. My debts to Margaret Milne, Helen Mason, Barry Brickell, the Perrins, Lucie Rie, Hans Coper, Trevor Hunt, Roger McGill and Raymonde Hawthorne are unrepayable.

All the things I do seem to relate; perhaps because it is me doing them, they have a private logic that defies any external scrutiny. They are not in separate compartments, they all interact and overlap. I subscribe to the Well Rounded Aesthetic Ideal, I guess.

Having been a self-employed potter most of my working life, I find the newer areas of theatre design and writing about film are similarly very time-consuming and labour-intensive. All my interests are visual. They all concern the drama of reactions to shape and colour and arrangement. They are all theatrical. There was a time when I suspected I only made pots to be able to display them.

Working on monthly magazine copy or an exhibition of pots is no different from working on a play, except that in the first two cases you are on your own. There are the same pressures and unalterable deadlines. The same themes flow through your work and the same processes of stylisation, fine tuning and attention to detail apply. The adrenalin rush generated by a first night, meeting a publication deadline or an exhibition opening is all the same. Previously having worked mostly with my eyes and hands, I now find the discipline of having to write 2000 words once a month and actually say something is good for the brain.

In all my interests, what the viewer gets is once removed from me. You read a review, you touch a pot or you see a design. You don't read, touch or see me; you do it to my work. I am a very private, behind-the-scenes person. I don't think I am a frustrated actor — but maybe I'm a frustrated director.

I have always been interested in simple, stark shapes as extensions of the traditional bowl and bottle forms. The limits to which definitions and taste can be pushed intrigue me.

All my work is thrown on a Talisman electric wheel. Most of the shapes I work in go against the natural organic tendencies of clay and gravity. You have to make up new techniques to get what you want. I will use

JP

BIOGRAPHY

1947 Born in Auckland
1966 Began night-school potting with Margaret Milne
1967 Built stoneware kiln with Grant Hudson
1970 Graduated from Auckland Teachers College
Member 12 Potters Cooperative, Auckland
1971 Received small electric kiln from Mavis Robinson
1972 Designed the 10th Annual Auckland Studio Potters Exhibition
1973 London, Royal College of Art
1975 Graduated MA, R.C.A., London
1976 Shared workshop with Ian Godfrey, Islington
1977 Returned to Auckland
1977–81 Director, Auckland Studio Potters Centre, Onehunga
1977–83 Designed the annual Fletcher Brownbuilt Pottery Award exhibitions, Auckland
1981– Film reviewer, *Metro*, Auckland
1983–6 Head of design, Theatre Corporate, Auckland,
Co-presenter, *Flicks* television series
1986– Resident designer, Mercury Theatre, Auckland
1987 Designed Fletcher Challenge Pottery Award exhibition, Auckland

Exhibitions

1967– Auckland Studio Potters annual exhibitions
1969– NZ Society of Potters annual exhibitions
Upstairs Gallery, Hamilton, with Grant Hudson
Member World Crafts Council
1972 30th Concorso Internazionalle della Ceramica d'Arte, Faenza, Italy
Christmas Show, Media, Wellington
1973 First solo show, New Vision Gallery, Auckland
1975 Degree show, Royal College of Art, London
Group show, Oxford Gallery, Oxford
Christmas show, Goswell Road Workshop, London
33rd Concorso Internazionalle della Ceramica d'Arte, Faenza, Italy
National Museum of Wales, Cardiff
1976 Heals, London, with Ian Godfrey
Mixed show, Upper Street Gallery, London
Group show, Third Eye Gallery, Glasgow
Group show, Tom Caldwell Gallery, Belfast

24 British Potters, travelling show, USA
1977 Oxford Gallery mixed show, Oxford
Porcelain show, Media, Wellington
Porcelain II, Alicat, Auckland
New Vision Gallery, Auckland
1977–80 Exhibited annually, Fletcher Brownbuilt Pottery Award, Auckland
1978 *Crafts New Zealand*, overseas travelling exhibition
Porcelain III, Alicat, Auckland
Media, Wellington
4 x 10 : Four Approaches, Peter Webb Gallery, Auckland
1979 Brooke Gifford Gallery, Christchurch
Blackfriars Gallery, Sydney
North Island Potters, Dowse Art Gallery, Lower Hutt
New Vision Gallery, Auckland
1980 The Craft Centre, Melbourne
Albany Village Pottery, Auckland
Domestic Wares, Alicat Gallery, Auckland
1981 Blackfriars Gallery, Sydney
New Vision Gallery, Auckland
Dowse Art Gallery, Lower Hutt
1982 CSA Gallery, Christchurch, with John Hadwen, weaver
Pots of Ponsonby, Auckland
1983 *Textures*, New Vision Gallery, Auckland
Basic Black: Twenty Bowls, Denis Cohn Gallery, Auckland
1984 *Porcelain — Four Potters*, 12 Potters, Auckland
Clay And Glass Az Art, Flagstaff, Arizona, USA
1984–6 Exhibited annually, Fletcher Brownbuilt Pottery Award, Auckland
1985 *Decorative Art*, 12 Potters, Auckland
1986 *Happy Birthday To Me*, Real Time, Auckland

Awards

1979 Merit Award winner, Fletcher Brownbuilt Pottery Award, Auckland
1980 Merit Award winner, Fletcher Brownbuilt Pottery Award, Auckland
1985 Merit Award winner, Fletcher Brownbuilt Pottery Award, Auckland

Collections

Auckland Institute and Museum
Pennsylvania State University, Pittsburgh, USA
Dowse Art Gallery, Lower Hutt
Manawatu Art Gallery, Palmerston North
Waikato Art Museum, Hamilton
Museum of Applied Arts and Sciences, Sydney
NZ Ministry of Foreign Affairs
Represented in private collections throughout the world

BOWL, 1987
Height — 19 cm. Oxidised porcelain copper and
brass, agate. Fired to 1240°C.
PHOTO — HOWARD WILLIAMS

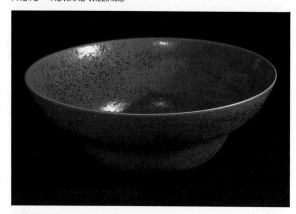

DOUBLE CURVED BOWL, 1987
Diameter — 23 cm. Oxidised blue crystalline
porcelain. Fired to 1240°C.
PHOTO — HOWARD WILLIAMS

anything to aid the process of getting there.
I am very Machiavellian when it comes to
masking tape and string. I tend to throw
blanks as finely as I can and severely turn
them into the precise shapes I intend. I use
metal kidneys most of the time and work on
any surface I can reach. I stretch and coax
rather than throw shapes. Bowls are always
turned inside and out. I am not interested in
the random and the spontaneous. I want to
be better than a lathe, more plastic than
plastic. I have a considerable failure rate at
all stages of the process. If you are not
losing work, you know you are not pushing
things far enough. I like working on a
tightrope and in areas I don't know anything
about.

I want the same control from glazing, but
here techniques vary. I don't dip or pour any
more because of overlaps and dribbles. I
spray mostly, but the Hobby Ceramics
glazes, by their very specialist nature, are
brushed according to the instructions on the
packet.

I use a few clays. I am looking for a
commercially prepared vitreous pale body
to fire to 1240°C in a 6 cu. ft electric kiln, but
this isn't always easy. Some I mix from an
excellent Steve Rumsey adaptation. The
Podmore porcelain is the best, but imposes
size restrictions, and careful drying is
needed. I wrap things in dry-cleaning bags
as soon as they get leather hard and
sometimes they sit for weeks equalising. I
turn at a dry, leather-hard state, often over a
few stages.

I have managed to standardise firing to
1000°C for stoneware and porcelain bisque
and low-temperature glazes, and 1240°C
for high-temperature bisque and stoneware
and porcelain glost.

ZIGZAG VASES, 1987 ▷
Heights — 19 to 23 cm. Oxidised stoneware with a
silicon carbide slip under a zinc matt glaze containing
copper carbonate, fired to 1240°C. Subsequently a
lead-chromium glaze is brushed on thickly and the
pieces refired to 1000°C.
PHOTO — HOWARD WILLIAMS

◁ GROUP OF HOBBY CERAMICS BOTTLES, 1987
Heights — 9 to 12 cm. Oxidised porcelain glazed
shiny black inside, fired to 1240°C. Subsequently a
commercial glaze was brushed on and the pieces
refired to 1000°C.
PHOTO — HOWARD WILLIAMS

CECILIA PARKINSON

PHOTO — ANNA CAMPBELL

If I could have chosen when to have been born, or better still, an era in which to have been an adult, I would have liked it to be the twenties or thirties. I am very fond of Art Deco design with its fresh, clear, crisp lines.

Working with clay is one of the most self-satisfying occupations one can find. There are so many avenues to take, and when you spend days testing clay and glazes, the potential outcome is unlimited.

In 1984 I was awarded an honorary degree in ceramics at the First World Triennial Exhibition of Small Ceramics, Zagreb, Yugoslavia. With a QEII Arts Council overseas study grant I was able to attend the conference that was held in conjunction with the exhibition. Travelling overseas to different countries, meeting and discussing with other artists the medium in which we work, helps you with your own personal philosophies about clay. Visits to Lucie Rie, a master potter in London, helped me a great deal in coming to terms with my inner feelings and the pottery I make.

At the moment I work solely in porcelain. Some of it is saggar fired, that is, the pot is fired within a pot with sawdust, metallic oxides, and sulphates, then fired in a gas kiln. For other pieces I use the agate technique, with silicon carbide and copper which forms crater-like swirls. The pieces are then glazed and fired in an electric kiln. I am experimenting with low-fired lead glazes. Some of these are fired in an electric kiln; others are fired in a gas kiln and reduced in a rubbish tin.

I like to have 'play' periods — just mucking around on the wheel, making different shapes. Sometimes, if I am lucky, I may come up with something I would like to take further. I am a person who needs change. I find I am always experimenting and trying something new.

1. and 2. Filling the saggar

CP

BIOGRAPHY

1963 Emigrated to New Zealand
1969–76 Worked with rattan cane, making baskets, and wrote a series of books on working with cane
1976 Began potting with Margaret Milne at the Auckland Studio Potters Centre
1979–81 Treasurer, Auckland Studio Potters Society
1979–82 Secretary, Auckland Studio Potters Centre
1979–82 Secretary, Auckland Studio Potters Society
1979–85 Member, 12 Potters Cooperative, Auckland
1980 Attended the World Craft Council Conference, Vienna
1982 Editor, NZ Society of Potters Newsletter
1984 Attended symposium in conjunction with 1st World Triennial Exhibition of Small Ceramics, Zagreb
1987 Member, Albany Village Potters Cooperative
Exhibition designer, Auckland Studio Potters annual exhibition
Advertising manager, *New Zealand Potter*

Exhibitions

1978– Auckland Studio Potters Society annual exhibitions
NZ Academy of Fine Arts annual exhibitions
1980– Exhibited annually, Fletcher Brownbuilt Pottery Award, Auckland
1981 *Earth And Fire*, Central Regional Arts Council travelling exhibition
The Bowl, Crafts Council of NZ exhibition, Wellington
1982 Solander Gallery, Canberra
1983 *New Zealand Arts* exhibition, Myers, Surfer's Paradise, Australia
World Crafts Council exhibition, Canada
New Zealand Ceramics Now, Suter Art Gallery, Nelson
41st Concorso Internazionalle della Ceramica d'Arte, Faenza, Italy
Pots of Ponsonby, Auckland
1984 1st World Triennial Exhibition of Small Ceramics, Zagreb, Yugoslavia
Clay And Glass Az Art, Flagstaff, Arizona, USA
John Leech Gallery, Auckland
1985 Museum Contemporary, Skopje, and ULUPUH, Zagreb, Yugoslavia
New Zealand Ceramics 1985, Suter Art Gallery, Nelson
1986 44th Concorso Internazionalle della Ceramica d'Arte, Faenza, Italy
New Zealand Potters, Gallery Eight, La Jolla, California
Elizabeth Fortner Gallery, Santa Barbara, California
International Gallery, San Diego, California
1987 Winstone Craft Biennale, Auckland

Awards

1982 Merit Award winner, Fletcher Brownbuilt Pottery Award, Auckland
1984 Honorary Degree, 1st World Triennial Exhibition of Small Ceramics, Zagreb, Yugoslavia

Collections

Auckland Institute and Museum
Suter Art Gallery, Nelson
Auckland Studio Potters Society
Southland Art Gallery, Invercargill
Private collections in New Zealand and overseas

Publications

Ceramica Moderna, Italy, 1986
Potters Manual, Kenneth Clark, UK, 1983

77

◁ DECO BOTTLE, 1987
30 × 18 cm. Porcelain. Barium matt glaze.
PHOTO — HOWARD WILLIAMS

GLAZED AGATE BOWL, 1985 ▷
12 × 18 cm. Porcelain with copper.
PHOTO — HOWARD WILLIAMS

SAGGAR-FIRED BOTTLE, 1986 △
15 × 10 cm. Porcelain
PHOTO — HOWARD WILLIAMS

◁ DECO FORM, 1986
18 × 12 cm. Porcelain. Low-fired lead glaze.
PHOTO — HOWARD WILLIAMS

SAGGAR-FIRED FORM, 1986 ▷
8 × 14 cm. Porcelain.
PHOTO — HOWARD WILLIAMS

RICK RUDD

My training in ceramics at Great Yarmouth and Wolverhampton colleges of art in England over a period of four years was inclined towards sculptural rather than domestic ware. My work from 1978 to mid 1986 was raku fired and each piece an exercise in line and form. Since then it has been more figurative, with inspiration taken from the human body, but still with the emphasis on form and line.

My materials are deliberately limited to three commercially prepared New Zealand clays, with grog added for texture rather than strength. At present I use only two glazes: a clear crackle glaze and the same one with 10 per cent commercial black stain added. This small range of materials is enough to give contrast between smooth,

BIOGRAPHY
1949 Born at Great Yarmouth, Norfolk, UK
1968–9 Foundation course at Great Yarmouth College of Art and Design, UK
1970 Worked with Mathies Schwarze, Numbrecht, West Germany
1973 Came to New Zealand
1978–80 President, Auckland Studio Potters
1980– Tutored numerous weekend and week-long schools throughout New Zealand
1982 Tutor for 2 months, Southland Community College, Invercargill
1986 Vice-president, New Zealand Society of Potters

Exhibitions
1975– Auckland Studio Potters annual exhibitions
1977–86 Exhibited annually, Fletcher Brownbuilt Pottery Award, Auckland
1978 *Four Approaches To Ceramics*, Peter Webb Gallery, Auckland
1979– NZ Society of Potters annual exhibitions
NZ Academy of Fine Arts annual exhibitions
1979–82 Annual solo exhibitions, Alicat Gallery, Auckland
1979 *North Island Potters*, Dowse Art Gallery, Lower Hutt
1980 *Handcrafts New Zealand*, Hastings Cultural Centre
1981 *The Bowl*, Crafts Council of NZ exhibition, Wellington City Art Gallery
New Directions In Ceramics, Dowse Art Gallery, Lower Hutt, and Waikato Art Museum, Hamilton
39th Concorso Internazionalle della Ceramica d'Arte, Faenza, Italy
1982 *Craft And Architecture*, Auckland Institute and Museum
Group exhibition, Blackfriars Gallery, Sydney, Australia
1983 *New Zealand Arts* exhibition, Myers, Surfers Paradise, Australia
The Bowl, Asian Zone of World Crafts Council exhibition touring to India, Pakistan, Thailand and Fiji
41st Concorso Internazionalle della Ceramica d'Arte, Faenza, Italy
New Zealand Ceramics Now, Suter Art Gallery, Nelson
New Vision Gallery, Auckland
The Great New Zealand Box Show, Crafts Council of NZ, Wellington City Art Gallery
1984 *Clay And Glass Az Art*, Flagstaff, Arizona, USA
1985 International ceramics exhibition, Taipei Fine Arts Museum, Taiwan
NZ Ceramics '85, Suter Art Gallery, Nelson
1986 *Pacific Link*, Expo '86, Vancouver, Canada
New Zealand Potters, Gallery Eight, La Jolla, Calif., USA
Albany Village Pottery, Auckland
1987 Winstone Craft Biennale, Auckland

Awards
1978 Winner, Fletcher Brownbuilt Pottery Award
1980 Merit Award winner, Fletcher Brownbuilt Pottery Award
1981 Winner, *The Bowl*, Crafts Council of NZ exhibition, Wellington
1982 Merit Award winner, Fletcher Brownbuilt Pottery Award
1983 Winner, New Zealand Academy of Fine Arts Caltex Oil Award
Merit Award winner, Fletcher Brownbuilt Pottery Award
Highly commended, *The Great New Zealand Box Show*

Collections
Auckland Institute and Museum
Waikato Art Museum, Hamilton
Dowse Art Gallery, Lower Hutt
Manawatu Art Gallery, Palmerston North
Robert McDougall Gallery, Christchurch
Southland Museum, Invercargill
Anderson Park Art Gallery, Invercargill
Hawkes Bay Art Gallery and Museum, Napier

heavily textured and shiny surfaces, with the natural colour of the clay showing in most pieces.

All my work is hand-built by a process of pinching, coiling and scraping. Spring steel scrapers are used to bring up the texture with the grog that has been added to the clay and certain areas are then smoothed for glazing later. Shapes evolve rather than begin as separate ideas, and much time is taken developing new forms to a satisfactory degree. The making process is very slow and several days can be spent on one piece.

The work is fired in a gas kiln to approximately 1050°C.

PHOTO — WANGANUI NEWSPAPERS LTD

RAKU NO. 900 ▷
Height — 40 cm. Pinched and
coiled.
PHOTO — CES THOMAS

ORANGUTANG, GORILLA AND
MANDRILL
Heights — 23, 30 and 23 cm.
Pinched and coiled.
PHOTO — CES THOMAS

RAKU NO. 901 ▽
Diameter — 12 cm. Pinched and
coiled.
RAKU NO. 926 ▽
Height — 25 cm. Pinched and
coiled.
PHOTO — CES THOMAS

(UNTITLED) △
Height — 125 cm. Grogged white
clay, pinched and coiled, fired to
1170°C.
PHOTO — CES THOMAS

KATHERINE SANDERSON

I grew up enjoying the freedom of a rural Taranaki township, later contrasted by high-school years spent in a Taranaki boarding school. My first contact with clay was at Teachers College where we were introduced to pottery — one kick-wheel. ('Have a go if you feel inclined'.) I don't remember a kiln.

Years later, married, with two children, I tried again at night classes and this time I caught on. Like most of my contemporaries, I became entrenched in production ware — plates, bowls, casseroles, all made in the back of the garage, with the reduction period of the oil-firing timed for night.

Frustrated by all the trials and much error and never achieving very satisfactory results, I pursued all avenues of knowledge — weekend schools, summer programmes, all the while lamenting the lack of a structured course for ceramics, i.e. one with technical information. Then my half of the garage burnt down — the hot wax left on while I was lunching inside with a friend — which necessitated, at last, a new shed — warm, light, pleasant, and with water laid on. With two friends I helped build a wood-fired salt kiln in the country and I discovered (or finally admitted) I was not a pyromaniac after all. They were — just as well!

Still trying to find a clay I felt more comfortable with, I began experimenting with flat raku pieces with impressed designs. Apart from the immediacy of the firing, what appealed most were the colours

and soft quality of the finished pieces, so I stopped making stoneware and began again, quite differently, with earthenware. I especially like the colour of the clay, and the terra sigillata sheen. My pots are mostly about myself and the pleasure I get from using these materials.

Now my kiln is a fibre-lined stainless-steel box, fired with gas. I am less concerned with the firing and can concentrate on the forms and the decoration, and I have accepted the fact that my work is largely experimental and probably always will be.

The pots are thrown in sections from Winstone's 1100 — a clay not without its problems, but I have stayed with it because I like the colour. After assembly, the pots are carefully smoothed with a steel rib. When they are bone dry I spray them with terra sigillata made from the same clay, buffing the surface as I go with a cloth of chamois leather. The colours are commercial stains mixed into a ball clay terra sigillata. The colours are painted on, building up the layers, then buffed. The pots are fired to 950˚C or 1000˚C.

Terra sigillata

3 kg clay
8 kg water
50 g Calgon (sodium polyphosphate)

On standing, the clay separates into three layers. The top, clear, layer is siphoned off, and the middle layer, which is the terra sigillata, is used.

1. Throwing the inner bowl of the pot — upside-down on a bat.
2. Throwing the bowl part of the pot — upside-down on a bat.
3. The base is thrown on a concave plaster former mounted on the wheel head.
4. The 'bowl', with inner bowl in place, is inverted on to the concave base. A heart-stopping moment while I find out if the 'bowl' will remain adhered to the bat while it is positioned on to the base.
5. The inner bowl is exposed and can now be smoothed.
6. Pots are carefully smoothed with a metal rib.
7. Pots are removed from the plaster former and placed on a collar for even drying. When dry they are sprayed with terra sigillata.
8. Sprayed with terra sigillata and being buffed with a chamois cloth as I go.
9. Terra sigillata coloured with commercial stains and applied with a brush.
10. It takes hours to apply the colours, building up the layers for the desired effect.

ALL PHOTOS — STAN JENKINS

JAR FORM, 1985
34 × 40 cm
PHOTO — STAN JENKINS

INNER BOWL FORM, 1985
26 × 42 cm
PHOTO — STAN JENKINS

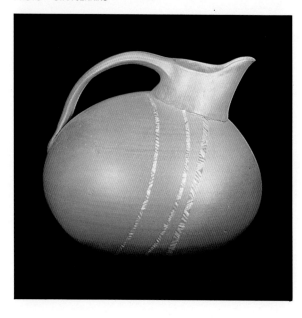

JAR FORM, 1985 ▷
34 × 42 cm
PHOTO — STAN JENKINS

BIOGRAPHY
Born in 1940
1958–9 Primary Teachers College,
Palmerston North
1978 Six-week course in abstract design with
John Ford
1980 President, Manawatu Pottery Society
1981 Brian Gartside workship — raku
NZ Society of Potters clay seminar with Don
Reitz and John Pollex
NZ Society of Potters delegate for Manawatu
1983 Selector, with George Kojis, for
Wanganui Pottery Society Annual Exhibition
1984 Selector for Hawkes Bay region for NZ
Society of Potters national exhibition
QEII Arts Council grant for fibre kiln construction
1985 Vice-president, NZ Society of Potters

Exhibitions
1979 *3 Potters*, invited exhibition, Manawatu
Art Gallery, Palmerston North
1981 Invited exhibitor, NZ Society of Potters
national exhibition
1982–5 Exhibited annually, Fletcher
Brownbuilt Pottery Award, Auckland
1982–6 NZ Society of Potters annual
exhibitions
1984 Selected by NZ Society of Potters to
submit work for 42nd Concorso Internazionalle
della Ceramica d'Arte, Faenza, Italy
1985 43rd Concorso Internazionalle della
Ceramica d'Arte, Faenza, Italy

Collections
Waldegrave Collection, Manawatu Art Gallery,
Palmerston North
Awatapu College, Palmerston North
NZ Academy of Fine Arts, Wellington
Govett-Brewster Art Gallery, New Plymouth
Teachers College, Palmerston North

JUG FORM, 1985 ▷
25 × 22 cm
PHOTO — STAN JENKINS

◁ JUG FORM, 1984
22 × 22 cm
PHOTO — LEIGH DOME

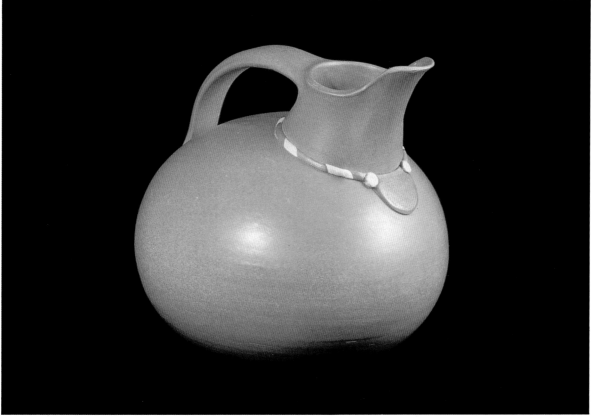

ROBYN STEWART

I like rounded forms. I find them satisfying to make, to touch and to look at. I spend many hours on each pot I make. Small pieces are pinched. Larger ones are coiled or slab built. Many are carved, the designs being influenced by those of my Celtic forbears, and of the country in which I live.

When burnishing, I use an Indian bloodstone, a traditional jewellers' burnishing stone.

All my pots are made from terracotta clay fired for 24—36 hours in a primitive firing using dung, grass and bark. The whole process gives me much satisfaction and pleasure, which I hope shows in my work.

Pots that influence and inspire me are neolithic, Chinese, Pueblo Indian and African.

BIOGRAPHY
1938 Born in Auckland
1975 Commenced potting at the Auckland Studio Potters Centre
1977 First pots were exhibited at the Auckland Studio Potters annual exhibition, after experimenting for 18 months with local clays, burnishing and dung firing
1982 Chosen as one of three craftspeople to represent New Zealand at the Commonwealth Arts Festival, Brisbane, Australia
1984 Established home and workshop north of Auckland, on the edge of the Waiwera estuary
1985 Exhibition designer, Auckland Studio Potters annual exhibition
1986 Consultant for the NZ Government in Lombok, Indonesia

Exhibitions
1978 Northland Society of Arts, Whangarei Guest exhibitor, Maori Artists and Writers Society, Auckland
1979 Blackfriars Gallery, Sydney
1980 Guest exhibitor, Maori Artists and Writers Society, Whangarei
1980—4 Exhibited annually, Fletcher Brownbuilt Pottery Award, Auckland
1981 *The Bowl*, Crafts Council of NZ exhibition, Wellington
1982 British Commonwealth Festival of Arts, Brisbane
1985 Dowse Art Museum, Lower Hutt
1986—7 Exhibited annually, Fletcher Brownbuilt Pottery Award, Auckland

Collections
Auckland Institute and Museum
Dowse Art Museum, Lower Hutt
NZ Ministry of Foreign Affairs

PHOTO — ANNA CAMPBELL

1. Drawing the pattern **2.** Carving **3.** Burnishing

◁ DUNG-FIRED BURNISHED POT,
1987
42 × 22 cm
PHOTO — GEORG KOHLAP

◁ DUNG-FIRED BURNISHED POT,
1987
22 × 28 cm
PHOTO — GEORG KOHLAP

THREE DUNG-FIRED ▷
BURNISHED POTS, 1987
PHOTO — GEORG KOHLAP

◁ DUNG-FIRED BURNISHED POT,
1987
44 × 24 cm
PHOTO — GEORG KOHLAP

SALLY VINSON

PHOTO — GIL HANLY

Domestic studio pottery amply describes the work that I have always made and will probably continue to make. I make pots for the domestic side of life, to contain and serve food, which is after all an essential part of the way in which we civilised people live. I have always tried to design the pots to fit the purpose for which they are required, while being aware of the potential decorative qualities that I can bring to everyday utensils simply because they are made by hand. I am happy that I have control over the work every step of the way.

Excuses for poor quality and bad design simply because the work is handmade have always appalled me. Human beings by their nature love to make objects, some useful, some decorative, and to combine the two has always seemed perfectly natural to me.

I see myself as a person in trade. For me, that means that I have sold what I make to earn a living from the business that these sales promote. Therefore I have had a responsibility to those who buy my work, in terms of a properly designed and executed product, an efficient service to the customer and good all-round business etiquette. I really enjoy the fact that making pottery earns me a living!

The work I make is described as 'majolica'. This type of pottery originated in Mesopotamia, Egypt and Persia, moving to the Mediterranean countries in the ninth century. Basically it is a medium-to-high-fired earthenware, specifically covered with a rich, lead-based glaze opacified with tin oxide and decorated on-glaze with rich oxide colours. In hot sunny Auckland, the

sally vinson

BIOGRAPHY
1939 Born in London
1955–7 Started pottery when attending
Birmingham College of Art at age 16
1957–60 Worked at Briglin Pottery in London
for three years after leaving Birmingham at 18
1960–3 When 21, gained place at Central
School of Arts and Design in London, to take
Diploma in Ceramics, which was gained 3
years later
1964–71 Set up workship in Greenwich and
worked there until leaving to come to New
Zealand. During this period taught at
Birmingham College of Art, Medway College of
Art and Central School of Art and Design,
London.
1971 Arrived in New Zealand and set up a
workship in Wellington
1973 Set up workshop in Devonport, Auckland
1981 Received Zonta Award and travelled to
Europe
1981–5 President, New Zealand Society of
Potters
1986 Committee member, Northbridge
Community Arts Council, Auckland
Treasurer, Auckland Studio Potters
Member of Advisory Committee on Craft,
Carrington Technical Institute, Auckland
Member of National Evaluation Crafts
Education Advisory Committee
QEII Arts Council short-term study grant to
travel to England to study decoration techniques

Exhibitions
1976 Alicat Gallery, Auckland
1980 Alicat Gallery, Auckland
1982 New Vision Gallery, Auckland
Guest Potter, Southland Potters Society,
Invercargill
NZ Society of Potters annual exhibition
1984 Guest potter, Wellington Potters Society
Exhibitor, Fletcher Brownbuilt Pottery Award,
Auckland
1985 Compendium Gallery, Auckland
1986 Guest potter, Tauranga Potters Society
Auckland Studio Potters
NZ Academy of Fine Arts, Wellington
Compendium Gallery, Auckland
New Vision Gallery, Auckland
Crafts Council of NZ exhibition,
Wellington
Spheres, NZ Society of Potters exhibition,
Southland Museum, Invercargill

Collections
1971 Work commissioned for the NZ Embassy
in Peking
1978 Work commissioned for the ministerial
suites in The Beehive, Wellington
1984 Boardroom dinner service commissioned
for Ministry of Agriculture and Fisheries,
Wellington
Work purchased by NZ Ministry of Foreign
Affairs; Government House, Auckland and
Wellington; Waikato and Southland Museums

ware I produce seems to be as appropriate as it is in the Mediterranean countries of Spain and Italy. The surface of the glaze is absorbent to the brush and I find decorating the pots a very satisfying part of the procedure.

It is hard to envisage my life without working with clay and producing useful objects. My life since I was 16 has always revolved around this activity, with brief interruptions for such events as having children! Not that they held up proceedings a great deal. Working in my studio at home enabled me to have the best of both worlds and a happy supportive family who in their turn have enjoyed the satisfactions that work has brought me.

The introduction of fulltime tertiary craft education in New Zealand has brought a change of direction in my work. As a tutor at Carrington Technical Institute I am able to put back into the system experiences gained in my training and in the workplace. Learning to be a craft worker will no longer be the hit-and-miss affair it has been in this country and we can look forward to a new generation of potters whose background will be both academic and practical. I am pleased to be part of this process, even though my own work in clay in the meantime will have to take a back seat.

THREE BLACK AND GOLD BOTTLES
Heights — 35 cm, 25 cm, 16 cm.
Earthenware. Black glaze and gold
lustre.
PHOTO — CES THOMAS

TEA SET ▷
Teapot, milk and sugar, 2 cups and
saucers. Teapot height — 25 cm,
including handle. Majolica.
PHOTO — CES THOMAS

SET OF THREE STRAIGHT-SIDED DISHES
Diameters — 25 cm, 22 cm, 18 cm;
Height — 26 cm. Majolica.
PHOTO — CES THOMAS

SALAD BOWL ▽
Diameter — 30 cm. Majolica (view
of outside design).
PHOTO — CES THOMAS

SHANE WAGSTAFF

I never did a single thing until I started making pots. I got into it through my mother, who was going to night classes, when I was about 14. She showed me what she had learned each time and I took it from there. Basically I spent about three years amusing myself with a pottery wheel. By the time I had developed any skills my mother had stopped potting altogether. We built a small oil-fired kiln in the backyard. It was terrible. It fired to cone 10 on the top and cone 7 on the bottom and it was only two feet high. From that I developed an interest in building kilns.

By the time I left school I was seventeen. Because I couldn't decide what I wanted to do, my parents allowed me to stay home and make pots until I could find a suitable job. I never found one, but I am still looking.

I had a lot of practical kiln-firing help from Fran Conquest. The following year she arranged for me to go and work with Barry Brickell. I was there for a few months and learned heaps about all sorts of things but when I left I realised just how much I had learned about potting. I then went to say hello to Jan Bell, who was working towards a firing. She asked me to stay and make some pots. I stayed a month and learned even more.

Then, through The Potters Gallery Cooperative in New Plymouth, I met Roger King and a year later I went to work in his studio. I worked there for 18 months, firing with wood but building a small LPG kiln there.

In 1983 I established a house and pottery of my own in Inglewood where I still live and work.

About four years ago I made a conscious decision to stop making traditional domestic ware because I was really bored with it. I hated glazing domestic ware and when I found that I could make and sell pieces that I had really enjoyed glazing, I decided to concentrate on decorative ware.

My main interest is in colourful and unusual glazing effects on simple forms, bowl shapes especially.

I use a fine white New Zealand clay fired in a natural-draught gas kiln. Most of my

ALL PHOTOS — ROGER KING

WORK IN PROGRESS

1. A basic form is thrown to which I often add an extra coil of clay at the leather-hard stage, in this case to gain extra height.

2. and **3.** The form is then re-thrown and given a semblance of its final shape by the use of stainless steel formers.

4. and **5.** Only after extensive trimming will the final form be revealed.

SW
Inglewood
N.Z.

work has been glaze-fired to the stoneware temperature of 1280°C, but I am currently experimenting with brightly coloured glaze stains at 1200°C.

All the pieces illustrated here were fired to 1280°C under neutral/oxidising conditions on a white clay. Colour variation was created by thickness of glaze.

2

4

3

5

◁ PLATE
Diameter — 24 cm. Barium
and copper glaze brushed on
inside.
Glossy black outside.
PHOTO — ROGER KING

TWO VASES ▷
Diameters — 11 cm; heights
— 15 cm. Glossy black glaze
inside. Barium and copper
glaze sprayed very thickly on
outside, causing glaze to run
during firing.
PHOTO — ROGER KING

BOWL ▷
Diameter — 16 cm; height —
17 cm. Glossy black glaze
inside; barium and copper
glaze sprayed outside.
PHOTO — ROGER KING

◁ PLATE
Diameter — 24 cm. Barium
and satin white glaze
sprayed on inside. Glossy
black outside.
PHOTO — ROGER KING

HOWARD WILLIAMS

I cannot really call myself a potter — I am not able to throw on the wheel — so ceramist, designer, artist, whatever, must be more accurate.

As a slip-casting pot maker, ceramic mural designer and maker, photographer, painter, violinist, author and magazine editor, I find no boundaries between all the art forms other than those drawn by materials and techniques used. All art forms are concerned with expressing ideas with line, form, balance, composition, texture and colour. If one has the ideas, it is a matter of learning the skills to handle the materials appropriate to the expression of each particular idea. Theoretically, time and

BIOGRAPHY

1935 Born in Auckland
1954–6 Trained as art and craft specialist teacher, Auckland and Dunedin Teachers' Colleges
1957 Itinerant art and craft advisor for South Auckland Education Board, based in Hamilton
1959–60 Travelled extensively in Europe, visiting potters and studying ceramics. Worked as a decorator in the Sevier's Studio Pottery, Hampstead, London
1961–4 Worked in the Kenneth Clark Studio Pottery, London, making slip-cast decorative earthenware, tiles and architectural murals
Took photographs to illustrate Kenneth Clark's book, *Pottery For Beginners*
1965–70 Operated from own studio in Northampton. Held many exhibitions of pottery, drawings and paintings. Taught adult classes in pottery and graphic design.
Commissioned for several architectural murals
1971 Returned (married with 2 children) to New Zealand and built a pottery studio/shop in Silverdale
1972–4 Executive committee, Auckland Studio Potters
1974 Wrote and illustrated *New Zealand Pottery Workbook*, published by Beaux Arts
1974–6 Executive committee, NZ Society of Potters
1975 Founding (and present) member of Albany Village Pottery gallery
1976–82 Editor of NZ Society of Potters Newsletter
1978 Shifted to present studio in Albany
1984 Became editor of the *New Zealand Potter*
Taught at many pottery workshops throughout New Zealand.
Has written articles and taken photographs for several magazines, also books, exhibition catalogues and pottery archives.

Exhibitions

1975 Alicat Gallery, Auckland
1976 Van Helden Gallery, Wellington
Guest exhibitor, NZ Society of Potters, Dunedin
1977–8 Alicat Gallery, Auckland
1982–4 *Crafts And Architecture*, Auckland Institute and Museum

Collections

Pottery and ceramic wall pieces have been bought for permanent collections by the External Affairs Department (now NZ Ministry of Foreign Affairs) for the New Zealand Ambassador's residence in Tokyo and the permanent collection of New Zealand art in Canberra, Australia.
Many pieces are in museums, private and corporate collections. Major works of architectural scale can be seen at the following buildings (several of these murals include weaving by fibre artists Anita Berman and Monika Schaer-Vance.):

Boardroom, National Mutual Insurance building, Shortland St, Auckland
Foyer, Marac House, New Lynn
Foyer, East Coast Bays City Council Offices, Browns Bay
Foyer, Booth, Sweetman and Wolf, Architects, Vincent St, Auckland
Fletcher Challenge House, Great South Rd, Penrose
Foyer, Reserve Bank of New Zealand, Customs St, Auckland
Boardroom, Development Finance Corporation building, Queen St, Auckland
Bank of New Zealand, Ponsonby
Foyer, Southpac Tower, Queen St, Auckland
Foyer, Aetna House, Symonds St, Auckland

At present (1987) I am working on a major commission of a 40-square-metre ceramic and water wall for solicitors Kensington Swan's building being erected in Fanshawe St, Auckland, and a ceramic mural for the foyer of the Royal Guardian Exchange in Derby St, Auckland.

money should have no bearing on the creative process. In practice they are the biggest obstacles to the expression and presentation of one's ideas.

In ceramics I prefer to work on large-scale architectural pieces. It gives ultimate satisfaction to have one's work permanently on display in a public place where many people will hopefully enjoy it over a number of years. I also like to share my ideas with others. This I can do with murals, but also in writing about and photographing pottery and in the compiling, editing and designing of the *New Zealand Potter* magazine.

1. Designing a mural

ALL PHOTOS — ANNA CAMPBELL

2. Working on 'Ice City' (Ceramics and perspex by Howard Williams; weaving by Anita Berman).

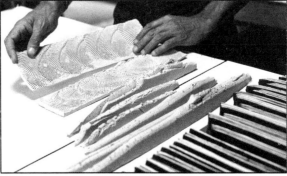

3. Rolled and wirecut earthenware pieces for murals

FIRE WINDOW, SOUTHPAC ▷
TOWER
Design and ceramics — Howard
Williams; weaving — Anita Berman
PHOTO — HOWARD WILLIAMS

RED SHIFT △
Design and ceramics — Howard
Williams; weaving — Anita Berman
PHOTO — HOWARD WILLIAMS

CEREMONY ▷
Width — 2 m. Design and ceramics
— Howard Williams; weaving —
Anita Berman
PHOTO — HOWARD WILLIAMS

◁ JUNCTION   Length — 1.5 m.
Earthenware.

102

MERILYN WISEMAN

I have been involved with clay for about ten years, spending the first few years learning to throw, discover suitable glazes, and to fire my wood kiln.

Gradually I became more and more interested in hand-building, playing around with forms which I could not throw on the wheel. It has been a slow process, teaching myself new techniques only because that was the way to solve problems and give form to the concept — a very satisfying way of learning about clay.

Hand-building cannot be hurried and allows time to work intuitively. I really enjoy that quiet involvement with each piece, although I find it frustrating that it takes so long to fill my kiln! I have got to know the clays that are sympathetic to the way I make and fire my work — clay that I can roll into slabs, adding fat coils which I beat, extend and play around with.

Changes and development in my work have been gradual, new ideas forming while I am working with clay rather than from some intellectual exercise outside the work.

Even though decorating, glazing and firing become separate, ordered processes, I think of them as an integral part of the making process and am very conscious in the early stages of the work of the part they will play in the finished piece.

I enjoy decorating with coloured slips —

BIOGRAPHY
Born Auckland
1958 Attended Elam School of Art for one year, then travelled to England to study at Goldsmiths College of Art
1962 Gained a National Diploma of Design
1963 Gained an art specialist teacher's diploma
1967 Returned to New Zealand. Became interested in clay and worked briefly with Jeff Scholes and Adrian Cotter.
1975 Established a pottery near Albany Built a double-chambered woodburning kiln
1982 Joined the Albany Village Pottery cooperative

Exhibitions
1982– Exhibited annually, Fletcher Brownbuilt Pottery Award, Auckland
1984 *Selected Northern Potters*, Compendium Gallery, Auckland
Clay And Glass Az Art, Flagstaff, Arizona, USA
The Pleasure Of Fire And Clay, New Vision Gallery, Auckland
1985 *Exhibition of Recent Work by Past Winners of Fletcher Brownbuilt Awards*, Pots of Ponsonby, Auckland
Flat Earth, 12 Potters Gallery, Auckland
Albany Village Pottery 10th Anniversary Exhibition, Auckland

Guest potter, Auckland Studio Potters annual exhibition
NZ Ceramics 1985, Suter Art Gallery, Nelson
Showcase II, Crafts Council of NZ Gallery, Wellington
1986 *Out Of New Zealand*, Santa Barbara, Calif.
Auckland Studio Potters Group show, Suter Art Gallery, Nelson
Pacific Link, Expo '86, Richmond Art Gallery, Vancouver, Canada
Guest exhibitor, Waikato Society of Arts, Hamilton
Ceramics '86, Govett-Brewster Art Gallery, New Plymouth
Auckland Studio Potters annual exhibition
Showcase III, Crafts Council of NZ Gallery, Wellington
1987 *Two Women*, joint exhibition with Robyn Stewart, Villas Gallery, Wellington
Winstone Craft Biennale, Auckland

Awards
1984 Winner, Fletcher Brownbuilt Pottery Award, Auckland
1986 Merit Award winner, Fletcher Brownbuilt Pottery Award, Auckland

Collections
Auckland Studio Potters Society
Waikato Museum of Art and History, Hamilton
Auckland Institute and Museum
Fletcher Brownbuilt collection
Private collections in New Zealand and overseas

painting and trailing them — applying them while the clay is still near-soft and the pot fresh in my mind.

The style of my work is closely bound to the way I fire. The unglazed areas of the clay I use which are exposed to the flyash can range in colour from soft apricot to vivid orange, and I enjoy the interplay between these surfaces and those which are glazed, and the overall softening quality that the wood ash produces.

PHOTO — ANNA CAMPBELL

SMALL BOX △
17 cm square
PHOTO — HOWARD WILLIAMS

PLATTER ▷
Diameter — 32 cm
PHOTO — HOWARD WILLIAMS

106

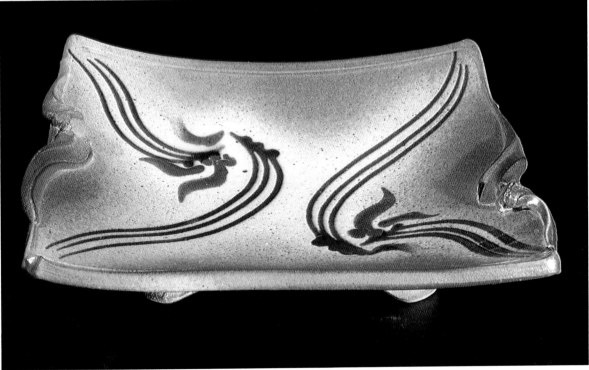

Glossary

ABSTRACT EXPRESSIONISM. A style known as 'action painting' and associated with the work of one of its initiators, American Jackson Pollock (1912–56).

AGATE. Ware made with two or more different clays which are only partially blended in the making process. They remain distinctively separate in patterns similar to agate stone.

AIRBRUSH. A sophisticated spray-painting system enabling the carefully controlled use of small amounts of inks, paints and solutions.

ANAGAMA TYPE. A traditional Japanese single-chambered, stepped kiln, usually fired with wood over a long period, from 3–12 days, during which time the ash deposits from the firebox are drawn through the chamber and build up on exposed surfaces of the ware to form a type of glaze.

ASH DEPOSIT. *See* Anagama type.

BALL CLAY. A highly plastic secondary (sedimentary) clay which fires to a pale colour. Its desirable working qualities make it the basis of most potting clays.

BALL MILL. A sealable horizontal cylinder, made from or lined with an abrasive resistant material, which can be mechanically rotated. The mill is loaded with the materials to be ground as well as porcelain balls and water.

BASE GLAZE. The simplest form of any glaze before additives such as opacifiers, colouring oxides or stains are added.

BISQUE (OR BISCUIT). Unglazed fired ware. In the New Zealand context this usually refers to the first firing of ware at a lower temperature than the subsequent glost firing.

BLANKS. Basic shapes which are later modified.

BRONGNIART'S FORMULA. A method of calculating the dry weight of solids in a liquid slip or glaze.

BURNISHING. The polishing of the surface of leather-hard clay by a smooth hard object such as a stone, the back of a spoon or a metal rib.

CARBONISING. *See* Smoked.

CELADON. Green to blue-grey stoneware and porcelain glazes coming from iron oxide in a reduction atmosphere.

CENTRE. Pressure applied to a clay ball on the potter's wheel to align it to run true.

CLAY. Decomposed granite and igneous rocks. *See* Ball clay, Earthenware, Fireclay, Porcelain and Stoneware.

COILING. Handbuilding by the continued adding of coils or snakes of clay and working them together.

CONES. Pyrometric cones are elongated triangular pyramids made of ceramic materials designed to melt and bend at specific temperatures in the kiln.

COPPER SULPHATE. A soluble copper salt.

CRACKLE GLAZE. The intentional use of the network of fractures in a glaze known as crazing, as a decorative feature.

CRATER. A pitted texture to a glaze caused by bubbles which burst and remain.

CROSS-DRAUGHT TUNNEL KILN. A horizontal kiln in which the hot gasses travel from the firebox through the ware across the chamber to the flue exit in the opposite wall.

CROWN LYNN. Trade mark of Crown Lynn Potteries New Zealand Ltd.

CRYSTALLINE. A glaze in which crystals have formed in the glassy matrix of the glaze by a process of devitrification which is aided by slowly cooling the kiln.

CUBIST. A style of art in which objects are presented to give the effect of an assemblage of geometrical figures.

DAMPED DOWN. The closing of the damper in the chimney exit flue, to slow down the rate of cooling of a firing.

DAMPER. An adjustable chimney baffle to control the flow of gasses passing through the kiln.

DAVID LEACH PORCELAIN. A clay body devised by David Leach for Podmores and Son, UK. It was the first commercially prepared porcelain clay generally available in New Zealand.

DECALS. Lithographic transfers printed with enamels or stains which are made permanent by firing.

DIESEL KILN. *See* Kiln.

DUTCH OVEN. Type of large firebox particularly suited to the efficient burning of wood.

EARTHENWARE. A porous pottery made watertight by a covering glaze.

ELECTRIC KILN. Kiln fired with electricity by heating resistance wire elements or rods.

ENAMEL. A low-firing glass used to decorate pottery.

ENGOBE. An American term for slip. *See* Slip.

FIBRE. A lightweight insulating material formed of a mass of thread-like crystals of fused silica and other compounds.

FIREBOX. The primary combustion chamber of a fuel kiln.

FIRECLAY. A refractory sedimentary clay usually associated with coal deposits.

FIRING DOWN. The technique of slowing the cooling of a kiln by allowing the temperature to drop by cutting back the heat input rather than turning it off completely.

FLYASH. Ash carried by draught through the kiln.

GAS-FIRED. A kiln fired with burners using natural gas, compressed natural gas (CNG) or liquid petroleum gas (LPG).

GLAZE. A layer of glass fused into place on a clay surface.

GLOST. The American term for glaze firing.

GRANITE. An acidic rock with a high silica content.

GROG. Ground, pre-fired clay added to a clay body and used to give texture, to assist throwing, to aid drying or to reduce shrinkage.

HAND-BUILT. Forming ceramics without a wheel, by coiling, pinching, slab-building or moulding.

HIGH-FIRED. Ware fired above 1200° Centigrade.

HOBBY CERAMICS. A phenomenon from the USA providing a commercial service where students without any prior experience or training may buy, finish and decorate slip-cast shapes with prepackaged materials.

HOT WAX. Melted wax used as a resist to prevent glaze adhering.

INLAYING. The filling of grooves cut into a clay body with another clay of a contrasting nature.

IRON. General name of compounds of oxygen and iron.

IRON SULPHATE. A soluble salt of iron.

KILN. A refractory box to conserve heat which must be capable of being heated to at least 600° Centigrade.

LEAD GLAZES. Glazes where the principal flux is a compound of lead.

LEATHER-HARD. A stage of the drying process when clay is rigid but still damp. It is the ideal state for pots to be turned, and other additions made.

LOW-FIRED. Ware fired generally below 1100° Centigrade.

LPG. *See* Gas-fired kilns.

LUSTRES. Metal salts suspended in an oil medium which, after firing, leave a thin metallic coating on a glaze producing iridescent effects.

MAJOLICA. Decorated, tin-glazed earthenware.

METAL KIDNEY. *See* Ribs.

MIDDEN. Prehistoric refuse heap, largely of shells and bones.

MOULDS. Porous plaster formers used to absorb the moisture out of wet clay or slip.

NATURAL DOWN-DRAUGHT. A kiln where the hot gasses are drawn over a bagwall and down through the setting of ware through holes in the floor and then to the flue. A tall chimney is usually necessary to give sufficient draw.

OIL MEDIUM. *See* Lustres.

ON-GLAZE ENAMELS. *See* Enamel.

OXIDATION. A clear kiln atmosphere with plenty of air intake.

OXIDES. A compound of an element with oxygen.

PINCHING. Method of forming a pot by the compressing action of fingers and thumb.

PODMORE'S PORCELAIN. *See* David Leach porcelain.

PORCELAIN. A vitrified white ware which may be translucent at higher temperature.

PORCELLANEOUS. *See* Porcelain.

PRIMARY AIR. The air which combines with the fuel to cause the initial combustion.

PRIMITIVE FIRING. The heating of pots without a kiln using cow-dung or other combustibles to make a bonfire.

PRODUCTION THROWING. Repetitive throwing of a number of similar shapes.

RAKU. A low-temperature earthenware technique involving a very rapid firing cycle.

RED IRON OXIDE. An insoluble compound of iron.

REDUCTION. A kiln atmosphere which is lacking in oxygen and takes it from the metal oxides in the clay and glazes.

REDUCTION PERIOD. The part of the firing cycle when reduction is taking place.

RIBS. Tools of wood, metal, plastic or bone used to smooth clay.

SAGGARS. Refractory boxes traditionally used to protect pots from direct contact with flames. Now they are used as controlled mini-atmospheres with sawdust and metal salts.

SALT-GLAZED. Ware glazed by the volatilasation of common salt, thrown directly into the kiln.

SECONDARY AIR. Air introduced to assist combustion beyond the actual source of the flame.

SIDE STOKING. Adding wood or other materials to the chamber of the kiln.

SILICON CARBIDE. An artificial compound of silicon and carbon made from baked sand and coke. It causes a cratering effect in glazes.

SILICA SAND. A refractory sand often used as a kiln setting material.

SLIP. A mixture of clay and water, often used with colouring oxides for decoration.

SLIP-CAST. The technique of moulding using liquid clay in porous plaster moulds.

SMOKED. The controlled, oxygen-free blackening of a clay surface caused by a saturation of unburned carbon in the pores of the clay, especially in raku and primitive firings.

SODIUM FLAME. The spectacular afterburn from a kiln which has had salt introduced.

SOLUBLE SALTS. Chemicals which dissolve in water.

SPECIFIC GRAVITY. The ratio of the number of times a substance is heavier than the same volume of water.

SPRING-STEEL SCRAPERS. *See* Ribs.

STAIN. Commercially prepared colouring pigments.

STONEWARE. High-fired, dense vitreous pottery.

TALC. Magnesium silicate (French chalk).

TERRA SIGILATTA. A slightly glossy surface caused by a fine colloidal slip.

THROWING. The action of forming pots on a rotating wheel using water as a lubricant.

TIN OXIDE. A metallic element used mostly as an opacifier.

TURNING. Removing unwanted clay to achieve a particular form.

VITREOUS. Fired to fusion point.

WAD. Refractory clay used to seal saggars or support shelves, etc. It can be removed after firing.

WHEEL. A rotating disc on which pots are formed. A wheel may be kicked by the foot or turned by a stick or a variable-speed electric motor.

WOOD ASH. The inorganic residue after the combustion of the organic structure of wood.

WOOD-FIRED. Ware fired with wood as a fuel, which has a characteristic quality due to the flyash present.

Index